BEING TRUE

Being True: How to Be Yourself at Work

Published in 2023 by Hardie Grant Books an imprint of Hardie Grant Publishing

Hardie Grant Books (Melbourne)
Ground Floor, Building 1, 658 Church Street
Richmond VIC 3121, Australia

Hardie Grant Books (London)
5th and 6th Floors,52–54 Southwark Street
London SE1 1UN, United Kingdom

www.hardiegrant.com.au

Hardie Grant acknowledges the Traditional Owners of the country on which we work, the Wurundjeri people of the Kulin nation and the Gadigal people of the Eora nation, and recognises their continuing connection to the land, waters and culture. We pay our respects to their Elders past and present.

A catalogue record of this book is available from the National Library of Australia.

ISBN 978-1-743799-57-4

Editing, design and pre-press production by Grammar Factory Publishing
Printed in Australia by Griffin Press

BEING TRUE

How to Be Yourself at Work

Hardie Grant

BOOKS

CASSANDRA GOODMAN

'When I developed IFS, I knew that I could only take it so far. So I'm thoroughly honoured that Cassie Goodman, a wonderfully talented teacher and writer, with extensive corporate leadership experience, has written this book that will inspire so many leaders to access their true selves and love their parts in ways that I never could. Cassie, I'm so grateful! *Being True* is a must-read for all leaders.'

RICHARD SCHWARTZ, PH.D., DEVELOPER OF INTERNAL FAMILY SYSTEMS, ADJUNCT FACULTY, DEPARTMENT OF PSYCHIATRY, HARVARD MEDICAL SCHOOL

'If you are ready to take the inner game of authentic leadership to a whole new level, you must read this book.'

PROFESSOR ALEX CHRISTOU, MANAGING DIRECTOR, THRIVE GLOBAL ASIA PACIFIC

'This book is a true game-changer, not just for leadership but for life.'

MARK EVARTS, DIRECTOR, TOMAHAWK RECRUITMENT

'What a relief to discover that good leadership flows from being myself, not trying to change myself.'

KELLIE KING, CEO, WOMEN IN TECHNOLOGY AWARD WINNER 2022

'If every leader read *Being True* and learned to take better care of their different parts, we'd totally transform the world of work.'

MELISSA BUCKINGHAM, PEOPLE EXPERIENCE DESIGNER, LEAPGEN

'*Being True* has changed the way I lead.'

ALLIE MACKAY, PSYCHOLOGIST & DIRECTOR, ALLIE MACKAY PSYCHOLOGY

'Being True is beyond amazing. This book is life-changing.'
BRIAR HARTE, HEAD OF ACCESSIBILITY,
LARGE AUSTRALIAN COMPANY

'Being True reminds us how important it is to lead as our authentic self – a self comprising many parts. Being True is a worthy companion to help you identify, recognise and understand which parts support you to lead with a stronger sense of self-worth, self-confidence and self-care. Cassandra reminds us what a joy it is to be true to yourself and move more comfortably and ably through your life with you at your side!'
KAREN STEIN, EXECUTIVE COACH, ICF PCC

'Cassandra guides us to understand the protective parts of ourselves, peel back our leadership armour and honour our core selves.'
NICK ELLEM, LEADERSHIP STRATEGY
MANAGER, TRANSPORT FOR NSW

'Being True is an invitation to create space to explore who we truly are as leaders and as people. It helped me to realise the importance of putting myself on my list of priorities. My emotional response to identifying my many parts took me by surprise – in a good way. It was a powerful experience.'
MOHINI SASHINDRANATH CPA, DEPUTY CFO

*'This book has given me the tools and the confidence
to heal my past and brighten my future.'*
CAROLYN HOWARD, CO-FOUNDER, PILATES 2GETHER

*'Cassandra is one of the most productive and passionate
thought-leaders I know. Her sense of purpose is palpable to
everyone who works and collaborates with her. Her book is a
must-read for my private coaching clients.'*
RENATA BERNARDE, HOST OF THE JOB HUNTING PODCAST

*'This book was exactly what I needed right now.
Being True is going to rock the world.'*
MIA BOWYER, CEO, ONE EARTH MARKETING

*'The paradox of Being True is that to bring our whole,
true self to the game, we need to recognise, own, make
peace with and tend to our different parts. I will never
look at Russian dolls in quite the same way!'*
RACHEL AUDIGÉ, BIAS BUSTER AND DIRECTOR OF SYSTEMATIC
INVENTIVE THINKING

I respectfully acknowledge the First Nations
people of Country throughout Australia and pay
my respects to Elders past and present.

I acknowledge the cultural and spiritual connection
that Aboriginal and Torres Strait Islander
peoples have with the land and sea.

May we learn from their ancestral ways to walk gently on
Country and to live more harmoniously with ourselves,
with each other and with the natural world.

You are welcome here.

With all your parts, and all your patterns.

There is space for all of you here.

I have faith in your true essence.

I trust in your innate goodness.

It is my hope that this book supports you

to have more faith and trust in yourself.

I dedicate this book to my two sons, Elliot and Zach.

In the words of Cyndi Lauper,

I see your true colours shining through.
I see your true colours
and that's why I love you.
So don't be afraid to let them show.
Your true colours ... are beautiful,
like a rainbow.

Contents

Contents

Knowing others is intelligence;
knowing yourself is true wisdom.
Mastering others is strength;
mastering yourself is true power.

LAO TZU

Dear Reader,

At the risk of things getting a little weird between us right off the bat, I want you to know that I have written this book for you. I know that may seem like a lot of effort for me to go to, and it was. But it was worth it.

So many of us convince ourselves that who we *really* are is somehow not enough. Not strong enough. Not smart enough. Not experienced enough. Not kind enough. Not educated enough. Not brave enough. Not good enough. Not worth enough.

But this is not true.

At this very moment, the very best of human nature is seeking to express itself through you in unique, powerful and important ways.

This book is an invitation to join me on a pilgrimage of self-discovery. To figure out who we really are and to better understand why we do what we do.

I hope that this pilgrimage empowers you to embody a more truthful, more vibrant expression of all that you are. I am honoured to be your guide and steadfast companion, and I'm ready to begin whenever you are.

Love,
Cassie
xx

INTRODUCTION

Remember that while there will be plenty of signposts along your path directing you to make money and climb up the ladder, there will be almost no signposts reminding you to stay connected to the essence of who you are.

ARIANNA HUFFINGTON

Introduction

I landed my first ever job as a cake shop girl at a bakery a few blocks from my family home when I was fifteen. The first thing I learned at the start of my first shift was that I was inconvenient – or more specifically, my name was inconvenient. I had not even finished tying on my apron when the bakery manager, Mrs Donaldson (a matronly, no-nonsense woman in her fifties), matter-of-factly informed me that my name would be changed to Sandy because there was already another cake shop girl called Cassie.

It was very clear that I did not have any say in this decision – nor about my new name. I remember feeling slightly upset by the unexpected realisation that my much-anticipated enrolment into the world of work required me to change my name. But without even a hint of quibble, I diligently complied. And so, my bewildering and ever-shaping pilgrimage into the working world began. At the time, I could never have imagined that I would spend the next three decades of my working life trying to figure out who the heck I was – often feeling pressured to be someone or something I was not.

A few years later, at the ripe old age of twenty-one, I contributed this quote to my university graduation yearbook: 'Do what you love and love what you do, and you'll never work a day in your life.' I still had no real understanding of the challenges I would face in the working world.

I am currently forty-seven. I have spent over three decades working for dozens of organisations ranging from that small family-run cake shop to multinational behemoths. I have held dozens of different leadership roles, progressing from looking after that small team of cake shop girls to being accountable for improving the health and happiness of an 86,000-person workforce as a global business executive. Along the way I have married, divorced, remarried, become a mother to two boys and lived in nine different homes across two continents. While I am certainly still learning, today I have a much deeper appreciation of the reality of working life and the perils of denying, hiding and suppressing who we really are in the pursuit of more gold stars, more status, more recognition and more money.

I am familiar with the emotional and physical exhaustion that comes from trying to achieve and appease your way to worthiness, chasing a shimmering mirage of enough-ness that perpetually remains just out of your grasp. I understand the heavy toll of not liking who you're being – at work and at home.

Today, I understand that true success is not just about loving what we do – it's about loving who we are *being* while we do it. An even more important discovery is that it's impossible to love (or even like) who we are being when we are not being *ourselves.*

I know for sure that wellbeing, performance and fulfilment all flow from being who we are – not changing who we are. And that there is a large and growing body of research that backs up this knowing.

Over the course of my global leadership career and through my work today as a coach, facilitator, consultant and trainer, I have observed first-hand that many leaders struggle with a sense of disconnection from their true selves.

Change only happens when individual leaders find the courage to do the inner work required to change the way they relate to themselves and, therefore, to others. As we acknowledge the hidden hurts underneath our harsh, extreme, judgemental or self-protective ways, it becomes possible to feel greater compassion, curiosity and understanding towards ourselves and each other.

This inner work is best approached in good company, and with gentle precision. It calls us to cultivate a deeper appreciation of who we really are at our core and to practise new ways to care for and lead the different parts of ourselves.

I have been sharing and refining the concepts I have distilled into this book with leaders around the world for many years. The more I work with these concepts, the more I am blown away by how they reconnect us to the truth of who we are and how they can restore our faith in ourselves and each other.

Cultivating a stronger connection to our true nature enables us to feel truly seen – and, in turn, truly see others. It fosters cultures of belonging and activates more of our individual and collective potential at a time when we most need it.

The ripple effect produced by the simple yet powerful principles and practices I share in *Being True* should not be underestimated. They hold the potential to empower and enable us to treat ourselves and each other with more acceptance, more care, more kindness, more patience and more respect.

As more leaders learn how to transform their inner experiences to become aligned with their true nature, more workplaces will become places of true belonging.

And wouldn't that be a wonderful thing?

I'M SO GLAD YOU'RE HERE

Would you like to better understand who you *really* are at your core? Do you sometimes think to yourself: Why did I do that? That's not who I really am! Do you often feel conflicted or torn, like part of you wants one thing, but another part of you wants something totally different? Do you sometimes convince yourself that feeling over-whelmed means that you are somehow not enough? Does part of you feel that self-care is selfish? Do you sometimes worry that having nasty thoughts means that you're a nasty person? Do you yearn to let your true colours shine, but can't find the courage to stand out from the crowd?

You are not alone, and you are in the right place.

Over four centuries ago, William Shakespeare wrote the line, 'This above all: to thine own self be true.' The wisdom of these words continues to resonate across time and cultures. There is no denying that living a life true to ourselves makes us happier and healthier, but the challenge, of course, is in the *how*. How exactly can we be true to ourselves when so often it feels like we must change or lock away parts of ourselves to survive?

Many people live their whole lives trying to change themselves to fit in, to please, to appease, to be liked and accepted. Sadly, it's been reported that the number one regret of the dying is not having lived a life that was true to themselves.

Choosing to avoid the whole messy (and perhaps scary) business of figuring out how to be true to ourselves is understandable. But if you're a leader it's not advisable, because if you want to acti-vate more of your unique potential and inspire others to do the same, your choices and actions must send the very clear message that: 'Around here, it's okay to be yourself.' Anything less and your colleagues won't feel they have permission to bring their whole selves to work.

But I'm guessing you probably already know this because you're reading my book. I'm going to assume that you're curious to under-stand what it *really* means to be true to yourself at work (and in life) and that you're open to playing with new ways of thinking that will empower you to do just that.

If you bring an open heart and an open mind to the principles and practices in this book, then what you'll learn (and unlearn) has the potential to transform the relationships you have with yourself, those you lead and even those you love. I will guide you to cultivate practices you can call on easily to feel more empowered to become the leader you want to be – the sort of leader only *you* can be.

FROM LONGING TO BELONGING

Places of false belonging grant us conditional membership, requiring us to cut parts of ourselves off in order to fit in. While false belonging can be useful and instructive for a time, the soul becomes restless when it reaches a glass ceiling.

TOKO-PA TURNER[1]

We all long to belong. When we feel a sense of belonging at work, we're more likely to perform to the best of our abilities, more likely to thrive and more likely to stay.[2] Research shows employees who feel like they belong are three and a half times more likely to be engaged in their work.[3] And yet, so many people don't feel truly seen, heard and accepted at work. Sadly, one in two people are not willing to be vulnerable at work,[4] two in five people say that they feel isolated at work,[5] and one in three people feel that they can't bring their whole selves to work and that they cannot be truly open about themselves.[6]

The problem, of course, is that working life can feel like one long masterclass on how to fit in by fixing or hiding the many ways we are somehow inadequate, inappropriate or inconvenient. The unspoken rule in many workplaces is some version of: 'Around here, it's smart to fit in.'

This means that many of us have two jobs. We have our regular job, which is hard. And then we have our second job, which is even harder. It's the job of pretending 'there's nothing to see here', when inside it's a very different story. The demands of this second job include suppressing, disowning, fighting, denying, hiding, numbing and ignoring the parts of ourselves we feel afraid to reveal at work. The parts of us that feel unsure, overwhelmed, different, frustrated, alone or afraid. Psychologists call this second job 'surface acting', and over time it takes a heavy toll on our health, our relationships and our performance. Prolonged surface acting has been linked to depression and anxiety, decreased job performance and burnout. In the words of award-winning researcher Francesca Gino, 'Going against our true selves by forcing ourselves to conform is exhausting and hinders our ability to perform well and fulfil our potential.'[7]

The good news is that there is an alternative to this inner battle. We can all be more ourselves at work by learning and applying practical, evidence-based tools that support us to stay connected to our true nature and take care of all the different parts of ourselves.

The model that underpins this book and my work at The Centre for Self-Fidelity is the Internal Family Systems model – also known as IFS. IFS is an evidence-based, paradigm-changing model of human consciousness that has been transforming lives for over three decades. The model was created by Dr Richard Schwartz, a faculty member of the Department of Psychiatry at Harvard Medical School. Dr Schwartz began his career as a systemic family therapist and an academic. Grounded in systems thinking, Dr Schwartz developed IFS in response to clients' descriptions of the various parts of themselves.[8] One of the foundational assumptions of the model is that the human mind naturally comprises many different sub-personalities or 'parts'. All of our parts have positive intentions, wanting to keep us safe and connected; however, our parts can be misguided in their strategies to achieve these outcomes. I will provide more context on the IFS model later in the book.

WHAT YOU'LL LEARN FROM THIS BOOK

This book is for you if you want to learn an evidence-based approach that will empower you to:

- Deeply understand who you really are at your core
- Better understand, appreciate and care for the different parts of yourself
- Experience leadership as something that flows naturally
- Cope better with strong emotions such as frustration and overwhelm
- Rekindle essential innate leadership qualities such as courage, compassion, creativity, curiosity, connectedness, vitality and playfulness
- Feel more energised and alive
- Love (or at least like) who you're *being*, not just what you do
- Give others permission to bring their whole selves to work

To meet these outcomes with you, I've divided this book into two sections. The first section covers five foundational principles you'll need to be true to yourself.

These five principles are:

- Belonging comes from being true to yourself
- Self-abandonment happens little by little
- Being yourself requires knowing yourself
- You have a core and many parts
- Being true to yourself takes playful practice

The second section of the book covers five simple yet powerful practices that you can play with in the flow of your everyday working life.

These five practices are:

- Discovering your inner team
- Understanding the key players
- Caring for your parts
- Remembering who you are
- Harnessing your essence

Along the way, I will share my own personal stories along with the stories of the many leaders I have had the honour of accompanying on their brave expeditions into their inner worlds. It is my hope that these stories will bring the concepts of *Being True* to life in memorable and meaningful ways.

WHY I WROTE THIS BOOK

The point is not to become a leader,
the point is to become yourself.
WARREN G. BENNIS

While for me writing feels more like productive play than it does work, writing a good book is certainly no small undertaking. So, why did I invest hundreds of hours (and even more teabags) into writing another book?

Well, in addition to my own personal experiences with the heavy toll of self-abandonment, I believe there are six compelling reasons why figuring out how to reconnect to our true nature is an important and urgent impetus for every single leader on the planet today.

Reason #1: Because we need to do much more to create safe workplaces

If you lead people or hold a role within an organisation that impacts the experiences other people have at work (which, let's face it, is *any* role), then employee health and safety is at the heart of your responsibilities. This responsibility means understanding and addressing the workplace factors that pose a risk to the mental health of your colleagues.

According to Deloitte,[9] ninety-five per cent of C-suite executives agree they should be responsible for employee wellbeing and that business leaders 'have a responsibility to break down the stigma associated with mental health issues, like stress and anxiety, to ensure everyone can thrive at work'.[10] However, research reveals that only fifty-six per cent of employees think their company's executives care about their wellbeing, while ninety-one per cent of the C-suite think their employees believe they care about it.[11]

Worryingly, levels of psychological safety are declining, with the latest research indicating that only three in ten people feel that their team is a safe space to be honest and bring up mistakes (down from four in ten three years ago). 'Poor workplace relationships' and 'harassment' are in the top three reported workplace psychosocial hazards. Over ninety per cent of workers who feel burnt out report experiencing poor workplace relationships.[12]

Part of the problem is that there are too many executives relying on simplistic gestures such as fruit boxes, one-off webinars and weekly yoga classes. Back in my full-time executive days, I spoke with an HR colleague about the opportunity I saw to do much more to address the high levels of work-related stress across our organisation. Genuinely perplexed, he replied, 'What do you mean we need to do *more?* We're now offering Pilates *twice* a week!' I distinctly remember thinking to myself, 'Houston, we have a problem.'

Research confirms the causal relationship between expressing one's true self and improved wellbeing.[13] The practices you will learn in *Being True* reduce the stress of surface acting, and feelings of 'uncleanliness,' which, in turn, reduces the risk of burnout.[14] The practices also dissolve the barriers to effective self-care by cultivating the skills to overcome patterns of over-working, unhealthy striving, proving and perfectionism. Greater clarity and confidence are also natural outcomes of the practices you'll learn. All these things directly contribute to the opportunity to underpin performance by maintaining healthy lifestyle choices and work-life harmony – another key factor in employee retention.[15]

I am disturbed by the narrow and shallow nature of the conversations happening around most boardroom tables about what it takes to provide psychologically safe workplaces. Providing a safe workplace is so much more than providing ways for your people to speak up. Fulfilling your ethical and legal obligations to provide a psychologically safe workplace requires leaders to both monitor and mitigate psychosocial hazards. There are so many different psychosocial hazards that can be present in our workplaces. These hazards include emotional conflict, role ambiguity, role overload, role conflict, task conflict, aggression, exclusion and discrimination.

So many of the psychological injuries inflicted on people at work happen because leaders have lost touch with the truth of who they are. So many leaders are burdened with deeply buried injuries of their own. And it's these old injuries that cause them to behave in ways that are unkind, cold, cruel, harsh, hyper-vigilant, competitive, discriminatory, controlling, judgemental, insecure or extreme.

I see so much unacknowledged trauma walking the halls of workplaces every day. And this is a safety hazard because hurt people hurt people.

Here is the inconvenient truth: Until we learn how to care for all the parts of ourselves, we cannot properly care for others. As more leaders find the courage to do inner work to heal the parts of them-selves that feel abandoned, hurt, afraid and alone, more workplaces become safer spaces for everyone.

Reason #2: Because we need to cultivate cultures of true belonging

Good people are leaving good jobs in record numbers. The concept of 'quiet quitting' is currently trending. Quiet quitting is just a new way to describe an experience you may already be familiar with: losing your 'give a sh#t'. Adam Grant summed up this latest workplace phenomenon when he said, 'When they don't feel cared about, people eventually stop caring.'[16]

We know that the best way to keep people engaged and to retain them is to ensure that they feel valued, seen and respected by their direct manager, and by their organisation.[17] For people to feel that they belong, they must feel they have permission to bring their true selves to work. They must feel valued and appreciated for who they are, not just what they do. As the research of Dr Brené Brown confirms, true belonging 'doesn't require us to change who we are; it requires us to be who we are.'[18]

Importantly, leaders *saying* that they value diversity, inclusion and belonging counts for nothing. The only way to give people permis-sion to be themselves at work is for leaders to go first. And the truth is that too many leaders are disconnected from their true nature at work.

When people feel a true sense of belonging at work, they are more likely to be deeply engaged in their work, to thrive, to perform, to be a positive influence on others and to stay. Creating workplaces where everyone feels like they belong is better for the health of the people who work there and for the financial health of the organisation.[19] That's a win for employees, for employers, for customers, for employees' families and for the communities in which all those happier, healthier, more fulfilled and more financially secure people live, work and play.

Reason #3: Because we need to wave the white flag

So many of us are at war with ourselves.

Because of the subtle but insidious pressures to fit in, over time, many leaders acquire the belief that who they *really* are is somehow inadequate, inappropriate or inconvenient. This means that many leaders have a secret battle waging inside of them because they feel uncomfortable being their true selves at work.

There are many who encourage this fear-fuelled inner fight. I am not one of them. Engaging in daily hand-to-hand combat within ourselves is corrosive to the body, mind and soul. These exhausting inner battles take a heavy toll on our health, our performance and our relationships inside and outside the workplace. If we continue to battle with the inner voices that constantly criticise and judge us, those same inner voices will continue to criticise and judge others.

Your ego is not the enemy. Yes, it is likely that you have inner parts that are protective, judgemental and extreme. But if you can trust in your own goodness, you'll discover that you have no 'bad' parts. All your parts, no matter how extreme or misguided, are driven by an intention to keep yourself safe and connected. We'll learn more about this soon.

When we wave the white flag and begin to care for our parts in the way they need to be cared for, our inner experience transforms from a battleground into a space of growth and healing.

Reason #4: Because we need to transform our inner experiences to transform our workplaces

We are all familiar with the shocking statistics around increasing levels of depression, anxiety and work-related stress, heartbreaking rates of suicide, and the global epidemic of burnout.

The thing that upsets me the most about the tremendous amount of human suffering and psychological injuries occurring in workplaces around the world every day is that so much of it could be avoided if only we knew how to treat ourselves and each other with more kindness, compassion, understanding and care.

While the health, wellbeing and psychological safety initiatives organisations are investing in are well-meaning, too many remain ineffective. In a nutshell, most organisations are attempting to solve complex problems with simplistic solutions. The co-creation of thriving organisations, where employees can honestly say they are happier and healthier because of where and how they work, requires business transformation and cultural regeneration. The biggest challenge with most organisational change programs is that they leapfrog the core change catalyst – transforming the inner experiences of leaders.

Workplaces transform only if leaders find the courage to transform their inner experiences, to understand and overcome the things that are getting in the way of them being caring, courageous, curious, playful, connected and creative. Without access to these innate qualities, leaders are not adequately equipped to sense, learn and respond their way through the complex, messy work of transformation and regeneration.

Reason #5: Because we need to restore faith in our goodness

I recently met a senior leader who told me, 'I never reflect or look inside myself.' My working (heartbreaking) hypothesis on why leaders resist doing inner work is that so many leaders have convinced themselves that they are somehow inherently flawed or 'bad'.

We come to falsely believe that, deep down, there is something 'wrong' with us – and that if we were to fully reveal this 'wrongness' to the world, we would be attacked, rejected and abandoned. People are afraid to search inside themselves because they're terrified of what they might find, and what it might mean.

Our mainstream definition of the human mind is fundamentally flawed because it assumes we are singular in our psychology. The truth is that we all have many parts. We need a new understanding of the human mind – one that recognises our natural multiplicity.

The Internal Family Systems model reveals that inside every person is an elaborate system of parts with a uniting core at its centre. This explanation of the human mind means that we can finally make sense of and normalise our ceaseless inner chatter, inner tension and the moments when we simply don't act 'like ourselves'.

By learning that those nasty voices in our heads do not accurately reflect who we really are, we restore our faith in our innate goodness. And this means we are more likely to find courage to do the inner work required to finally begin to understand who we really are at our core, bear witness to the burdens we carry, heal our past hurts and learn how to treat ourselves (and each other) with more compassion, patience, acceptance and understanding.

Importantly, embracing our multidimensionality opens the possibility of coaching and leading ourselves (or, more specifically, our 'parts'). This new understanding of self gives us permission to become curious towards the less empowered, fearful, frustrated parts inside of us (and others) that can cause us to 'act out'. It helps us to stay tethered to our compassion in moments when we (or others) are engaging in problematic behaviours.

Reason #6: Because we are running out of time

So many of us are sleepwalking through our days, feeling deeply disconnected from ourselves, each other and the world around us. When we abandon ourselves, it hurts. Matt Licata PhD, a psychotherapist, captured the nature of this hurt when he wrote, 'We turn from ourselves in difficult times. When we abandon ourselves we often fall down the rabbit hole of dissociation, denial, shame, judgement, and blame and lose touch with the valid, human, and honourable inner experience that longs for our attention, curiosity, and care.'[20]

Now, more than any time in the history of humankind, we are in desperate need of true leaders. Jean Houston said it better than I ever could: 'We are among the most important people to have ever lived. We will determine whether humankind will grow or die, evolve or perish. We will need a gathering of the potentials of the whole human race and the particular genius in every culture if we are going to survive our time.'

We desperately need more leaders who can empower us to harness our individual and collective potential, and who can inspire us to sense, learn and respond our way through the complex challenges we are navigating together.

TRUE LEADERSHIP

There is no shortage of 'how-to' leadership models. Google 'how to be a good boss' and you'll get almost two billion results. If you want to read a book on leadership, you have over 100,000 to choose from. And yet, research reveals that only thirty-five per cent of employees feel inspired by their boss.[21] So, it's clear that more knowledge and more leadership frameworks are not the answer.

One of the shortfalls of many of the current approaches to leadership development is that they focus on the acquisition of new knowledge rather than on putting into practice our most powerful ways of being. We are searching *outside* ourselves for answers that can only be found *inside* ourselves. We are striving to imitate instead of figuring out how to better access and activate what's innate.

Much of the current advice on leadership is based on the flawed assumption that good leadership is about learning and implementing a 'best practice' model of leadership. In other words, to be a good leader you must learn and adopt a 'standard' set of skills or capabilities. Of course, there are technical skills competent leaders need to get under their belts, such as commercial acumen. However, all the technical skills in the world won't make you a true leader.

I would like to offer an alternative model of leadership – TRUE leadership.

Being a TRUE leader means that you:
*T*rust in your innate leadership potential, know how to *R*eassure yourself, deeply *U*nderstand yourself and can *E*mpower yourself in moments that matter.

And, as a natural outcome of these practices, TRUE leaders also:
*T*rust in the innate leadership potential of others, know how to *R*eassure others, deeply *U*nderstand others and can *E*mpower others in moments that matter.

Becoming a TRUE leader is more about unlearning than it is about learning. It's about activating the innate qualities of our essential nature as humans – qualities such as creativity, compassion, connectedness, clarity, confidence, playfulness, discernment and courage. And now, more than ever, we must tumble and polish the brilliant jewels buried deep inside each and every one of us. We must find the courage to do the inner work that will empower and enable us to step into more of our innate leadership potential.

THE UNDERPINNING MODEL: INTERNAL FAMILY SYSTEMS

IFS is one of the most innovative, intuitive, comprehensive, and transformational therapies [to] have emerged in the present century.
DR GABOR MATÉ[22]

As previously mentioned, the model that underpins this book and my work at The Centre for Self-Fidelity is the Internal Family Systems (IFS) model. IFS explains that we are not singular in our psychology, and that the voices in our heads are just the different parts of ourselves in conversation. IFS has been proven to be effective in the treatment of trauma recovery, addiction, depression and more.

My life has been a quest of self-discovery. I have chanted in incense-filled ashrams, done yoga headstands at dawn, skydived, bungee-jumped, karate-chopped through thick wooden planks and completed marathons and triathlons. I have attended dazzling no-expense-spared leadership development programs in Dubai, Prague, London, Barcelona, Arizona, Hong Kong, Melbourne and Sydney. I have had the privilege of learning from many gifted speakers and teachers at live events, including the Dalai Lama, Malala Yousafzai, Dr Brené Brown, Sir Richard Branson, Simon Sinek, Dr Kristin Neff, Dr Martin Seligman, Johann Hari and Dr Susan David. I have completed in-person training with great teachers including Dr Stuart Brown, Dr Rick Hanson and Tal Ben-Shahar. I have completed extensive training in Mental Health First Aid, mindfulness, positive neuroplasticity, design thinking, lean thinking, systems thinking, time-line-therapy and neurolinguistics. I have invested in many sessions with psychologists, psychotherapists and counsellors. I have spent countless hours in small rooms and cafes being coached, counselled and mentored. I have also explored alternative forms of healing, including reiki, art therapy, dance therapy, singing therapy, past-life regression therapy and hypnotherapy.

After all of this, it is hard to put into words how it felt when I finally discovered IFS. It was an experience of relief, validation, liberation and exhilaration. There were tears. IFS enabled me to clearly understand who I am at my core. It deeply validated what I already knew and gave me a framework for the conversations I was already naturally having with my coaching clients about the hurt underlying their problematic behaviours.

Over the past few years, I have been trained as an IFS-informed coach. I have also worked deeply with IFS coaches and therapists in my personal journey to being true to myself. I have experienced more personal insights, growth and transformation over these last few years than I did in the prior thirty years combined.

To my knowledge, this is the first ever book to explore the application of the IFS model specifically in the context of leadership development and the important work of psychological safety, inclusion and belonging at work.

In many of the podcasts and interviews Dr Richard Schwartz does, he tells the story of how his clients taught him about IFS when he was a family therapist in the 1980s. Richard explains how he came to work with families who had children suffering from bulimia. At the time, he was using a structural family therapy approach. Richard's clients did not get better using this approach, so out of frustration he began to ask why. To his surprise, his clients intuitively started talking about the different parts inside them. They would describe how, when something bad happened, their inner critic would attack them. That attack would bring up another part of them that felt totally worthless, empty, alone and young. These feelings were so terrifying that a bingeing part within them would come to the rescue and turn them into an unfeeling eating machine. They explained that while there was a lot of relief in that, afterwards the critic would attack them again for being a pig, followed by their worthless part resurfacing. And so, the binge would repeat. Many of these clients reported being trapped in this vicious three-part cycle for days.

This discovery was particularly intriguing to Richard because it mirrored the sequences of family interactions that he had studied when attaining his PhD in Family Therapy. What was even more intriguing was Richard's next discovery. He found that he could guide his clients to interact with their parts and that the parts were eager to tell their stories through images, memories and the impressions of thoughts. Through many more years of working with clients to illuminate, navigate and heal their inner worlds, the IFS model was developed.

IFS: Goals and Assumptions

The overall goals of the model are:

- To achieve balance and harmony within our internal system.
- To differentiate and elevate our 'core self' so it can take its place as the natural leader in our inner system.
- To access the talents of our many different parts in non-extreme ways.

The foundational assumptions of the model include the following:

- The human mind is naturally comprised of 'parts'; collectively these parts form our inner 'system'.
- Our parts interact with us, with the world around us and among themselves.
- All our parts have important 'jobs' to do in our inner system to keep us safe and connected.
- There is no such thing as a bad part. All parts have good intentions; however, they can be extreme or misguided in their tactics.

- The goal is not to eliminate, fight or suppress any of our parts, but rather to help them find positive roles to play within our inner system.
- Everyone has a core self that can (and should) lead our internal system and care for our parts.
- The core self is the grounded centre from which we experience the world. It is where our most positively powerful qualities reside.
- The core self encompasses many positive leadership qualities, such as confidence, compassion, connectedness, courage, playfulness, discernment, presence, patience and perspective.
- When we form a connection to our core self our parts can change rapidly – and so can long-held patterns of behaviour.[23]

HOW TO USE THIS BOOK

You must be the one to do or undo whatever it takes to activate your own furiously prolific heart.
BROOKE MCNAMARA

At the end of the day, the only person who can give you permission to step into a more truthful and vibrant expression of yourself is you.

As an IFS-informed coach, all the work I do rests on a basic assumption that we each have within us the wisdom we need to heal, to grow and to thrive. As we restore faith in our true nature, we come to trust that everything we need is already inside us. As a result, we become more attuned to the ways that our true nature can be blocked or restricted.

In this book, I am offering you expert guidance and steadfast companionship on the path to reconnecting with the natural leader inside you.

Being true to yourself at work is so much more than understanding your strengths, values, goals and development opportunities. Honouring who you authentically are flows from an understanding and acceptance of your many parts and a deep appreciation of who you are at your core.

Leaders who become more comfortable being themselves at work cultivate a clear, dynamic sense of the specific and unique ways that human nature blends and expresses itself through them. They also come to understand how their core self can be distorted and blocked by both internal and external factors.

I have worked hard to distil the contents of this book down to only what is essential. I did this so that the book would be easy to read and apply. I suggest that you keep this book close, so you can come back to it whenever you need a little help to remember and reconnect with who you are.

There are a couple more things you can do to help ensure you experience the many benefits *Being True* has to offer:

Give yourself the gift of focus

The first thing you can do as you start reading this book is give yourself the rare and precious gift of focus. Our attention spans are getting shorter and shorter. In any one moment there are often dozens of things competing for our attention. Maintaining our focus on any one thing for any length of time has become incredibly challenging. Despite the enormous and growing assault on your attention, make a conscious decision to minimise distractions as you are working your way through *Being True*.

Bring a beginner's mind

I also encourage you to bring what Zen Buddhists call a 'beginner's mind' to the experience of reading this book. You can bring a beginner's mind through an attitude of openness along with a deliberate dropping of expectations and preconceptions.

The practice of *Being True* is about shedding what no longer serves you. What you are seeking is already here, inside you.

These words from Dr Shefali encapsulate this idea beautifully: 'What you are here to reclaim, you had it once. You had it as that child who knew its might ... That child to whom it never once occurred that they were lesser than. That you had to become something to be happy. That you had to do something to prove your worthiness. You were that child who was complete, whole, significant, purposeful, connected, present. You were that child.'[24]

Don't go it alone

While the work of inner discovery is work only you can do, that does not mean you have to go it alone. I encourage you to think about finding a friend, colleague or family member to be your buddy on this exploration of your inner world. Travelling In good company means you're far more likely to keep going. You'll also have someone you can reach out to if things get tricky, and you'll have someone who's looking out for you. The other big benefit of having a buddy is that, if you choose carefully, they may act as a gentle mirror for you. A key success factor in improving self-awareness is receiving feedback from people who you know have your best interests at heart *and* who are willing to tell you the truth about how you sometimes show up.[25] Another option is to join my group coaching program. You'll find more information about this in the Support section of the book.

Get help if you feel you might need it

Some of the concepts I will share in *Being True* may cause feelings of disorientation. The process of updating our beliefs about ourselves can go to the core of our conditioned identity.

This book is not a substitute for medical support, and I implore you to talk to a mental health professional should you even suspect you need help. I know for sure I would not be where I am today without the psychologists, psychotherapists, counsellors, therapists and coaches who have supported (and continue to support) me.

There may be times when the support and guidance of an IFS-trained coach or therapist would be beneficial. A good coach or therapist can support you to illuminate and make sense of your inner world.

PRINCIPLES

Intelligence is traditionally viewed as the ability to think and learn. Yet in a turbulent world, there's another set of cognitive skills that might matter more: the ability to rethink and unlearn.

ADAM GRANT

OVERVIEW OF THE FIVE PRINCIPLES

Here is an overview of what we'll learn (and unlearn) in this next section on the key principles that underpin *Being True*.

Belonging comes from being true to yourself.	We'll bust the myth that fitting in is the pathway to belonging and discover that real belonging comes from *being* who we are, not *changing* who we are.
Self-abandonment happens little by little.	We'll discover that, as humans, we tend to change ourselves in 'tiny movements', not 'sweeping pivots'.
Being yourself requires knowing yourself.	We'll rethink what it means to be self-aware and learn that true self-awareness requires a more accurate understanding of the human mind.
You have a core and many parts.	We'll challenge the false belief that we are singular in our psy- chology to reveal that we all have many different parts and a uniting core self.
Being true to yourself takes playful practice.	We'll learn that embodying the truth of who we are requires an ongoing, moment-to-moment, playful practice of remembrance and reconnection.

Belonging comes from being true to yourself

Because true belonging only happens when we present our authentic, imperfect selves to the world, our sense of belonging can never be greater than our level of self-acceptance.

DR BRENÉ BROWN

Brené Brown once shared this personal insight: 'I feel I belong everywhere I go, no matter where it is or who I'm with as long as I never betray myself. And the minute I become who you want me to be in order to fit in and make sure people like me is the moment I no longer belong anywhere.'[26] This really hits home for me. For many years I believed that abandoning parts of myself was the only way to succeed as a leader in business. Very early in my executive career I worshipped the book *Nice Girls Don't Get the Corner Office*. Every morning I scraped my hair back into a tight, neat bun. I wore only collared shirts and tailored pants to work. I worked hard to keep my (somewhat cheeky) sense of humour in check to conform to the mould of a 'serious executive'. I was quick to dish out well-meaning but completely misguided advice to younger female colleagues, like suggesting that they needed to reconsider wearing their hair down if they wanted to be taken seriously.

Looking back, I cringe.

My ideas about how to feel like I belonged at that executive table were so deeply flawed. It's no wonder I always felt like I was playing dress-up and struggled with feeling very nervous so much of the time.

Today, being a man-impersonating woman sitting in a corner office feels more like a nightmare than a dream. I understand that being myself is the only way to feel like I really belong. Instead of my clothes being a costume, uniform or part of my 'armour', today my clothes celebrate the truth of who I am. Because I am far more comfortable in my own skin and far more at ease about being myself, I feel more at ease at any table. My consulting work means that I am a frequent visitor to executive tables. Even though some might consider me an outsider in this setting, I feel at ease and experience a sense of warm connection with the people I work alongside.

Think about the best leader you have ever worked with or for. Someone who really inspired you to go above and beyond. Someone who brought out the very best in you. Chances are this leader was not someone who spent their working days stiffly toeing the party line. If I were a betting person, I would wager that there were moments when you saw this leader struggle, that they could ask for help, that they had quirks, that their realness and their humanity was a big part of what made them a great, inspiring leader.

One of the strongest headwinds against cultivating cultures of belonging is pressure to betray ourselves to fit in. Because we are social creatures, we tend to comply with social norms or unspoken rules. We succumb to subtle (and not-so-subtle) pressures to hide our true selves at work to ensure we are a good cultural fit. When we do this, a sense of belonging eludes us. Research confirms that belonging is being part of something bigger than us, but it's also the courage to stand alone and to belong to ourselves above all else.[27]

While we may *think* that fitting in is the pathway to belonging, it's not. A real sense of belonging comes from *being* who we are, not *changing* who we are. Our sense of belonging starts from within. Embracing all our parts and honouring our essence is the gateway to experiencing true belonging.

Self-abandonment happens little by little

We shift ourselves not in sweeping pivots, but in movements so tiny that they are hardly perceptible, even in our view. Years pass before we finally discover that, after handing over our power piece by piece, we no longer even look like ourselves.

ALICIA KEYS

A single acorn can grow into a tiny, twisted bonsai or a towering, mighty oak tree. Both organisms share the same DNA and potential. The only difference is that the bonsai's growth has been diminished through root constraint and branch pruning.

Even though we might like to believe that we are somehow immune to our environments, we are not. Our inner worlds, our working worlds and our personal worlds shape the expression of who we are.

I have worked with thousands of good people over the years. Sadly, too many of these good people were living what Henry David Thoreau has described as 'a life of quiet desperation'.[28] For those of us who work in an organisation, there are many invisible 'forces' at play helping and hindering our capacity to really be ourselves. Our

experience at work and our mindset are influenced by the organisational culture, unspoken rules, our direct manager, our peers,
our colleagues and other leaders within our organisation. The truth,
however, is that the most diminishing forces are often the thoughts
we think. Or more specifically, the thoughts our *parts* think.

Given the many invisible forces that influence us at work and in
life, it is easy to conform, little by little, only to suddenly realise
one day that we no longer remember who we really are or what
we really believe anymore.

Often, we conform in ways that are small and subtle, driven by our
desire to fit in or by internalising other people's incomplete and
inaccurate assessment of our potential. But, over time, our choices
accumulate. We conform when we mould ourselves to the expectations of others or to perceived 'ideals' that we buy into. We conform
in a misguided attempt to belong.

The world of work can encourage you to squeeze yourself into small
spaces where it thinks you best fit. Over time, you can begin to
believe you should fit into these small, confined spaces. These small
spaces can take many forms.

Perhaps you have crunched yourself down to squeeze into the
footsteps of your parents. Maybe you have reined in your individual sense of style to comply with the dress code deemed to be
business appropriate by the powers-that-be in your organisation.
Perhaps you have been conditioned to prioritise the list of values
espoused by your organisation over your own core values. Perhaps

you have found yourself biting your tongue in meetings and leaving the hard questions unasked and unanswered. Perhaps you have limited the way you think about your own potential to the contents of your two-page job description. Perhaps you feel forced to comply with your company's preferred work hours or work location, even though they feel stifling. Perhaps you have learned not to expand your sphere of influence to a level that exceeds the shadow of your insecure manager. Perhaps the 'us and them' politics of your workplace means that you suppress your natural desire to connect and collaborate with others. If you're a mother, perhaps you crunch down the yearning to do big, meaningful work in the world to conform with society's traditional expectations that your life should tightly orbit the lives of your partner and children. If you work for a larger organisation, perhaps the drive for simplicity, standardisation and order is extinguishing your individuality.

Choosing to abandon parts of ourselves under the pressure to conform or fit in can become our default setting and cause us to go unnoticed, untested and unchecked. Over time, small choices can accumulate. Suffering can occur. Potential can be dulled and diminished. Our vitality and sense of agency can slowly drain away.

Whenever we allow constraining factors to suppress the expression of our uniqueness and potential, without challenge, we are potentially doing ourselves (and the world) a great disservice. When we understand that, as humans, we tend to change ourselves in tiny movements, not sweeping pivots, then we can bring more awareness to the day-to-day choices we make.

Unlike an acorn, we can all exercise some degree of freedom about how and where we choose to grow. With this awareness and freedom, we can assertively claim the space and the nourishment we need for our roots to spread, our branches to extend and our leaves to unfurl. We can all take proactive steps towards living a fuller expression of ourselves. We can all have wide-awake awareness of the nature of the environments we choose to plant ourselves in. As we find the courage to unfurl into our fullness, we feel inspired and uplifted. And we give others permission to do and feel the same.

PRINCIPLE 3:

Being yourself requires knowing yourself

Knowing yourself is to be rooted in being, instead of lost in your mind.

ECKHART TOLLE

If you were to ask someone who they really are, their answer would most likely be some version of, 'Well, umm … it's complicated.'

One of my coaching clients, Bob, came to realise that there was an explosive, protective part of him that was activated whenever he felt weak (or when the possibility of feeling weak was an imminent threat). Often, in important meetings at work, when the stakes were particularly high, Bob would be overcome with the feeling that he was about to explode with anger. Sometimes, when the pressure was too high, he did explode. This behaviour was a stark contrast to Bob's core self. When Bob was at his best, he was a calm, caring, deeply empathetic leader who was naturally attuned to what the situation called for.

Through our coaching sessions, Bob came to see a clear connection between his childhood experiences of being made to feel 'weak and stupid' by his troubled father and the 'job' of his 'Volcano Part'. Bob came to understand that the job of his Volcano Part was to protect him from being overwhelmed by the fear and sadness of his most vulnerable parts. The way it did this job was through explosive anger – at any cost.

With awareness, courage and practice, Bob got much better at recognising the early warning signs in his body that his inner Volcano Part was being activated by feelings of weakness. These signs included clenching his jaw, tightness in his shoulders and rising heat in his face.

Strong emotions carry very important messages – they can tell us a great deal about the fears and survival strategies of our many different parts. By cultivating the courage and the skills to listen to and decipher these messages, we illuminate and make sense of our inner worlds.

It was hugely empowering for Bob to understand and begin to care for the frightened little boy inside him, and as a result to turn down the heat of his inner volcano. Bob will never (nor should he ever try to) get rid of his Volcano Part. There are still times when Bob experiences an inner surge of anger. However, these experiences are becoming less frequent, less extreme and, when they do happen, Bob recovers much faster.

CULTIVATING TRUE SELF-AWARENESS

For many of the leaders I work with, their first step towards being true to themselves is figuring out who the heck they really are, because it's hard to be true to yourself if you're not clear on who you really are. For many people, this first crucial stepping-stone feels messy and scary. Often, leaders tell me that they have spent so long pretending to be someone else at work that they have lost touch with who they really are. Plus, because we all have so many different voices in our heads, it can be really confusing to try to figure out which of these voices represents the real us.

While most people believe they are self-aware, self-awareness is an extremely rare quality. And, contrary to popular belief, self-aware-ness does not increase naturally with more experience. It's also worth mentioning that the least competent people tend to be most confident in their ability.[29]

Sometimes, the obstacle that gets in the way of figuring out who we really are is that those pesky inner voices manage to convince us there is something fundamentally wrong with us, and we're petrified by the prospect of confirming these suspicions.

To make matters worse, our fear and resistance are being exacer-bated by a fundamental flaw in the way we think about our self and, therefore, our self-awareness. This flaw is the assumption that we are singular in our psychology – that there is just one self to get to know. This assumption is misleading and unhelpful. There is a hidden, complex system of parts inside each of us wanting to be discovered.

At the centre of this system of parts is our true essence – our core self.

Self-awareness has traditionally been defined as 'the will and the skill to understand yourself and how you are perceived by others'.[30] In traditional approaches to self-awareness, the goal is to see yourself in the same way others see you.[31]

The key limitation I see with this way of thinking about self-awareness is that it does not help us to show up more often in ways that are aligned with who we really are.

So, I would like to offer up an alternative definition of self-awareness. This new definition recognises our innate goodness and our multiplicity, and supports us to be good leaders.

I define true self-awareness as the compassionate cultivation of a deep understanding of our true nature, our core self and our many different parts.

The experience of *really* getting to know ourselves sometimes feels like taking the lid off a can of live worms. Despite this, there are many benefits of cultivating true self-awareness.

It makes us better leaders

Self-awareness has been shown to be the most important capability for leaders to develop.[32] It is the biggest predictor of leadership success. People who report to leaders with good self-awareness are more likely to feel more satisfied with them as leaders and see them as more effective in general.[33]

It's good for us and for those we lead

When we see ourselves clearly, we are more confident and more creative.[34] Greater levels of self-awareness have also been linked to greater levels of job satisfaction, and to leaders' dedication to their staff. These positive outcomes flow down to the leaders' direct reports.[35]

It's good for business

Organisations with self-aware employees perform better financially.[36] People who have good self-awareness have been shown to make sounder decisions, build stronger relationships and communicate more effectively. They're less likely to lie, cheat or steal. They're also more likely to perform well and get promoted.[37]

The good news is that with focus and practice, and a little coaching, true self-awareness is something we can all develop. This book will help you get there.

PRINCIPLE 4:

You have a core and many parts

When we simply turn our attention inside, we find that what we thought were random thoughts and emotions comprise a buzzing inner community that has been interacting behind the scenes throughout our lives.

DR RICHARD SCHWARTZ

As a way of introducing this fourth principle, I invite you to imagine the following scenario while also noticing what's happening in your body.

Your company is undergoing (another) major restructure. Your boss has decided not to take on board your suggestion that the first step is to have one-on-one conversations with everyone who will be impacted, and he has sent an all-employees email announcing the restructure. The rumour mill is in over-drive. Your top-performing team member has suddenly become very active on LinkedIn, and another has told you that they're feeling very anxious. This is making you very nervous about meeting the next key milestone of a large project you're accountable for delivering.

Your boss calls an urgent meeting with you to talk about what's going on and what to do about it. As the meeting progresses, your boss's lack of awareness of and empathy for those impacted by the restructure becomes very apparent. You start to feel like you're in a scene from *The Office*. You're working hard to play it cool, but when your boss expresses his annoyance at all 'the kerfuffle about first-world problems' you can no longer hide your frustration. An eye-roll escapes.

Noticing your body language, your boss asks if there is something you would like to share, and you take a deep breath to say...

'Thanks so much for asking. Allow me to explain exactly what's going on for me right now. So, there's this part of me that hates you right now for putting us in this situation. Then there's this other part that's angry about having to work for someone who is quite clueless about the impact these sorts of changes have on people. Then there's this part of me that just wants to fast-forward to 8.00 pm so I can eat pizza, drink wine, scroll through social media and go online shopping to buy stuff I don't need. And if I'm being *really* honest, there's also a very vulnerable part of me that's terrified because they believe that if I can't get my project back on track, I'm completely and utterly worthless. Oh, wait, there's more ... I just noticed a part that is judging me for thinking all of this and another part that is shaming me right now for oversharing. But you know what? Deep down, I really do believe that we are both good people just doing the best we can in difficult circumstances.'

How did imagining this scenario make you feel?

Of course, in a situation like this one, when our boss asks us if there is something we would like to share, we'll usually say something much closer to, 'Oh, no. Nothing.'

So, is it possible to navigate moments of inner turmoil such as this one in a way that's both honest *and* discerning? Authentic *and* professional? Can we open to the possibility that we have many parts *and* keep our jobs? The answer is yes. Not only can we embrace all the different parts of ourselves and keep our jobs, when done skilfully, it can make us much better at them.

It may be helpful to think of your parts as versions of yourself that are too young and too inexperienced to drive.[38] With practice, compassion, curiosity and patience, we can get to know our parts and learn how best to care for them. Over time, we can help them to trust in us and to see that things go better where we (our core selves) are in charge. Once this self-leadership is established, we can support our parts to play more appropriate and helpful roles in our inner system. Over time we can build a powerful inner alliance.

UNDERSTANDING YOUR ESSENTIAL NATURE

Your essential nature contains many positive and powerful qualities. These are the qualities of good leadership. Your essential nature is the core of who you are. It's your most valuable resource – a natural, renewable source of leadership, energy and vitality. You might like to think of it as the person beneath the 'personality'.

Our parts exist to keep us safe and connected; however, they can be misguided, clumsy or extreme in how they achieve these outcomes. When we are not being hijacked by our parts, we naturally have a good connection to our core self. Through this connection we access the qualities of our essential nature.

Unlike our parts, our core self is never seen by us. It is the witnessing 'I' in our inner world – the aspect of us that does the observing.[39] While our core self has no agenda, it does have an intention. That intention is to 'bring harmony, healing, balance and connectedness to any system it encounters'.[40] Your true self is the home base from which you can embody your most powerful leadership virtues.

With practice, your core self emerges as the natural leader or coach of all your different parts. The relationships we nurture with our different parts facilitate the empowerment and harmonisation of all the players in our inner system.

The qualities of your essential nature include being:

- Courageous
- Compassionate
- Calm
- Confident
- Creative
- Connected
- Clear

- Curious
- Playful
- Vital
- Present
- Patient
- Self-aware
- Discerning

When you read the above list, you might find yourself thinking that you do not possess some of these qualities. Rest assured, this is not true.

All these qualities exist inside of you, but some of them may be dormant, diminished or dulled. Just like seeds, even if some of these qualities have been dormant for a long period of time, they can still be activated. This is what we'll focus on in Practice 5: *Harnessing your essence*.

These qualities are enduring and indestructible. Some of them might be on pilot-light setting, but they can never, ever be extinguished. In the words of Dr Richard Schwartz, your true self 'can be temporarily obscured, but it never disappears'.[41]

The key ingredient that empowers us to gain the trust of our many parts and to coach and lead them is our connection to our core selves. By drawing on our innate leadership qualities, we can meet and welcome the parts of ourselves that have been working away in the dark for decades, with a genuine sense of curiosity, compassion, understanding, patience and appreciation.

YOUR ESSENCE

The qualities of our shared essential nature as humans blend and express themselves through you in a way that is unique to you. You have a way of being that only you can be. No other human on the planet expresses the qualities of our shared essential nature in the exact same way you do. Your essence is as unique as your fingerprint. Here is how Carol Sanford describes what essence is, and why it is so important:

> 'Essence is what makes every living system and being unique and it is the source for ongoing and life-giving creativity in your life. When we lose sight of it, we can more easily feel lost in who we are and what we are doing with our lives ... When people are persuaded to conform, their essences are overtaken by personality traits, and the characters they play take centre stage, nudging out their true selves. In order to develop the capability to recognise and engage with essence – our own and others' – we must hold it in mind and pursue its living expression in all of our efforts.'[42]

YOUR PARTS

We all have many parts. Multiplicity is the inherent nature of the human mind and our parts reflect a natural, adaptive response to a challenging world.

Every major school of psychology recognises that people have different parts. These parts may be referred to as sub-personalities, ego states, energy systems, inner-critics, schemas, saboteurs, cognitive distortions or states of mind. Throughout this book I will be using the term 'parts' to refer to the natural 'sub-personalities' that exist within all of us.

At some level, you intuitively understand the concept of having many parts. Have you ever been invited to a friend's party and thought, 'Part of me really wants to go because I don't want to miss out, but another part of me just wants to stay home, order pizza and watch a movie'? In a situation like this one, perhaps the part that wins out is the one that dreads the idea of telling your friend that you would rather stay home than come to their celebration, and so you get dressed up and go. Perhaps after you arrive at the party, you notice your energy shift as your outgoing, fun-loving life-of-the-party part awakens and you end up having a great time.

Dissociative Identity Disorder (DID), previously less accurately referred to as Multiple Personality Disorder, is a complex psychological condition that stems from a combination of factors, like extreme trauma in early childhood. DID is characterised by the presence of two or more 'split' personalities that have no awareness of each other. In the case of DID, a person may not be aware that they're behaving inconsistently. People living with DID may have items they don't remember buying or friends they don't recall meeting before. In contrast, people without DID are aware of their inconsistencies even when they are very polarised. For example, I want to go, and I don't want to go; I want to be close, and I am terrified of being close. DID is extremely rare, affecting less than one per cent of the population.[43] However, 100 per cent of people have multiple parts of themselves.

Our parts don't reflect some sort of dysfunction or calcified pathology. Rather, they are protective and adaptive responses to the challenges we have faced and the hurts and disappointments we have experienced in our lives. Our thoughts are the inner dialogue of our different parts. And often, the way our parts speak to us is way more disempowering than it is empowering. If we spoke to other people the way we speak to ourselves, it would be called emotional abuse.

We might see our parts as younger versions of ourselves, or we might experience parts as body sensations or urges. Some examples might include: The Chocolate Monster Part, The Wine Lover Part, The Shop-a-holic Part, The Shouty Mummy Part, The Withdrawn Part or The Volcano Part. Sometimes, people experience and express their parts as animals, objects or interesting characters. I worked with a client who discovered a Little White Mouse Part whose job it is to maintain a stash of salty, sugary snacks for when they feel the urge to self-soothe with food. Another client once identified a Boxer Part whose job it is to fight for what is right.

Your parts are very hard-working. They are the invisible inner team responsible for running your daily life, for helping you to be successful and for keeping you safe and connected. While all your parts play important roles, often, their go-to survival strategies result in negative long-term consequences. When we look within, we're likely to discover that some of our hardest working parts are exhausted and depleted. Our parts know that their go-to strategies are not working but lack the resources and sense of safety to adopt new roles within our inner system.

Every single part of you holds a positive intent for you, even if their actions or effects are counterproductive or cause problems in your life. This means that there is never any reason to fight with, coerce or try to eliminate a part. The aspiration of the practices you will learn in this book is to cultivate internal awareness, connection and harmony. The goal is to empower all of your parts to play more helpful, more resourced roles in your inner team.

The good news is that, over time, you can help your parts to trust in your core self as their natural, unifying leader. By harnessing your innate curiosity and patience, you can cultivate a relationship with all parts of yourself that is grounded in acceptance and appreciation. When we gently illuminate our parts, help them to meet and, over time, trust in the core self as their natural leader, we restore our inner harmony and create an inner alliance.

Before we take a closer look at the different parts that dwell inside you, I invite you to reflect on these questions:

- What new possibilities might emerge if you could extend compassion and curiosity to all your parts (and the parts of others) based on the understanding that having many parts is natural, universal and beneficial?
- What would it mean to trust that beneath all your inner chatter lies an indestructible core of goodness?
- What if the pathway to good leadership and true belonging is *being* yourself, not *changing* yourself?
- What if everything you need is already inside you, waiting patiently for you to notice?

MAPPING YOUR INNER SYSTEM

No two parts are the same, and all your parts are unique to you. Having said this, it can still be very helpful to understand the broad 'job categories' that parts typically fall into. Many different frameworks and tools exist to classify parts.

The tool that resonates with many of my clients is my Inner Alliance Map (shown on the page opposite). This map, based on the IFS Model[44] defines three distinct types of parts: *Manager Parts*, *Distractor Parts* and *Injured Parts*.

Let's explore this map. We'll start by taking a closer look at your different parts and the roles they play in your inner system, beginning with understanding your Injured Parts.

Injured Parts

The first category of parts can be described as *Injured Parts*. These parts have experienced pain and hurt in the past and, as a result, have become burdened with difficult emotions such as fear, shame, loneliness, sorrow, rejection, anxiety, worthlessness, powerlessness or anxiety.

We all have Injured Parts. Ironically, it's our efforts to protect these old injuries that can inadvertently inflict pain on ourselves and others.

Our Injured Parts can carry heavy, sometimes debilitating beliefs, such as, 'I am not worthy,' 'I am alone,' 'I am unlovable,' 'I am not safe,' 'I don't belong,' or 'There is something wrong with me.' Because of

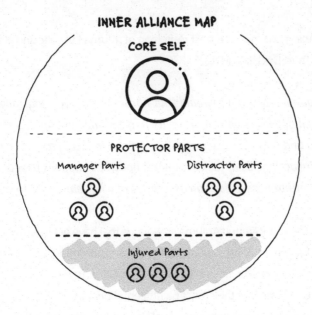

INNER ALLIANCE MAP

CORE SELF

PROTECTOR PARTS

Manager Parts

Distractor Parts

Injured Parts

these burdens, the Injured Parts of ourselves are not functioning in their natural state. They do not have good access to the qualities of our core self. For example, a part that carries a lot of shame and fear will not have access to our innate playfulness or curiosity.

As Toko-pa Turner explains, 'Whatever the particulars of your first estrangement, you will have felt the rift being torn between who you really are and who you had to be to survive. And so begins the work of moulding our qualities into this more acceptable version of ourselves. Over time, these efforts at "passing" as normal become all too successful, until even we begin to forget our true nature.'[45]

It is worth talking briefly here about what trauma is because there is so much unacknowledged trauma walking the halls of every work-place every single day. The origin of the word trauma is a Greek word meaning 'wound'. The best definition of trauma I have found is this one from Dr Gabor Maté:[46]

Trauma is a psychic wound that hardens you psychologically ... then interferes with your ability to grow and develop. It pains you and now you're acting out of pain. It induces fear and now you're acting out of fear. Trauma is not what happens to you, it's what happens inside you as a result of what happened to you.

So, we can think about trauma as wounds that have not been tended and have not yet been healed. We all have untended wounds. We can sustain these injuries in so many ways. Often, my coaching clients share with me that their most painful emotional wounds come from unexpectedly careless moments of deep humiliation, abandonment, betrayal or shame involving people who loved them the most. Often, these injuries are caused by moments that they see as so insignificant that they're sure their loved ones have no recollection of them. And yet, something very specific about the way these moments made them feel has stayed with them, often for decades.

Perhaps the reason these moments cut so deep is that we do not see them coming – we are completely blindsided by them. The shock of these moments can make us feel like the rug has been pulled out from under us. It might be the burn of the humiliation or the sudden belief that our deepest fears are true. It could be something as small as the way someone looks at us or turns away from us in a moment when we so desperately need to know we are safe and loved.

So, we all have Injured Parts. To function and keep up appearances, our inner system attempts to lock these parts of ourselves away in the darkest depths of our consciousness. Therefore, Injured Parts can also be called *exiles*. Our inner system wants to keep these injured, vulnerable parts protected and locked away because of the fear that their hurt, pain and sadness might be overwhelming.

To protect us from the pain carried by our Injured Parts, our inner system creates another category of parts – known as *Protector Parts*.

Protector Parts

All Protector Parts have the same goals: to keep Injured Parts exiled and to protect us from 'dangerous' feelings of shame, fear, sadness, guilt, pain and anger. Protector Parts are hard-working, have good intentions and take their jobs very seriously. However, they can often be extreme or misguided in how they fulfil their duties.

As you get to know your parts, you may observe that their way of handling things often brings about the exact opposite of what they are so desperately seeking. It can be a life-changing insight to realise that the parts of ourselves that are working so hard to protect us from pain are inadvertently causing us to experience pain.

Protector Parts employ one of two different strategies to achieve their goal of protecting our Injured Parts. So, depending on what strategy they adopt, Protector Parts fall into two further sub-categories – *Manager Parts* or *Distractor Parts*.

Manager Parts

Let's first take a closer look at how our Manager Parts do their job of inhibiting the potentially overwhelming feelings of our Injured Parts.

Manager Parts are the parts that run our day-to-day lives. These parts commonly employ strategies such as: striving, controlling, evaluating, caretaking, over-achieving, rationalising, perfectionism, hyper-vigilance, people-pleasing and judging.

Manager Parts change when the Injured Parts they protect are cared for and begin to heal. When our Injured Parts release their burdens, our Manager Parts can find new roles in our inner system. By helping our Manager Parts to relax and open space, we can gain permission to form relationships with the Injured Parts they are protecting. From here, we can help our Injured Parts begin to trust in the core self once again.[47]

Let's take a look at five examples of Manager Parts:

The Controlling Part

A part that has a strong need to take charge and stay in control. This part is strong-willed and may tend to be competitive or confrontational. They may feel anxious or impatient when things are not going the way they want them to go. This part craves certainty. Their deepest fear is that others will get close enough to see they don't have all the answers.

The Judgemental Part

A part whose job it is to find fault with self, with others or with situations. This job requires them to constantly identify what is 'wrong'. They may replay past hurts and mistakes over and over while being hyper-focused on what 'went wrong', or what people 'did wrong'. They may feel guilty, disappointed, resentful and ashamed. They may believe that people need to be pushed or punished to learn and change. Their deepest fear may be that they will make the 'wrong' decision.

The Hyper Achiever Part

A part that is relentlessly chasing the ever-elusive mirage that they can somehow achieve their way to being worthy. Their sense of self-worth and enough-ness is heavily dependent on external achievements, success, recognition, validation and status. They have an insatiable thirst for accomplishing things but never feel satisfied. They experience little joy or satisfaction from their accomplishments. Perhaps this part feels stuck in patterns of proving, competing and unhealthy striving that push you to the brink of exhaustion or beyond. Their greatest fear is not being enough.

The People Pleaser Part

A part that suffers from a sense of over-responsibility for others and an under-responsibility for self. They put aside their own needs to gain acceptance and affection by saving, rescuing, helping or flattering others. Their greatest fear is not being needed. They have a strong need to be liked and may need frequent reassurance. They may experience feelings of resentfulness towards others and may be prone to exhaustion and burnout.

The Keeping Up Appearances Part

A part that feels like it needs to 'keep up appearances' at any cost. For example, this part might show up as a Shouty Mummy Part who is convinced that their children's 'bad behaviours' mean that they are a complete failure as a parent and their kids are spoiled brats. Even though they hate themself for it, they find themself shouting at their kids in a desperate attempt to curb their behaviours. This part's greatest fear is being rejected for not being good enough.

Distractor Parts

Now that you have a better sense of Manager Parts, let's look at Distractor Parts. This family of parts also springs into action when your Injured Parts are at risk of being exposed. Their self-appointed job is to distract from the feelings of vulnerability through strategies designed to numb, suppress or extinguish difficult or uncomfortable emotions. Their mission is to protect your overall system from being overwhelmed. These parts can also be called 'Firefighter Parts' because their primary job is to 'hose things down' when we have unpleasant inner experiences. They may fulfil their duties in several different ways, including over-working, over-exercising, over-eating, binge-watching TV, mindless social media scrolling, shopping, drug or alcohol use, or even self-harm.[48]

The more I work with the principles and practices I share in *Being True*, the more familiar I become with how my parts can pull me away from my core. This empowers me to be more honest with myself about why I sometimes feel like I need to feel less.

I marked another trip around the sun as I was finishing this book, and I made the decision to un-invite alcohol to my birthday celebrations. This was kind of a big deal for me, not because I am a big drinker, but because alcohol has been an unquestioned part of my celebration (and commiseration) rituals for almost thirty years.

Through work I have done with my parts, I came to see that the choice to drink has rarely come from my wisest self. Sure, sometimes I consciously make the choice to savour a good glass of wine with good food and friends, but most of the time (if I'm being honest with myself) drinking is about feeling less of something.

In my teenage years (when I was so very desperate to be cool), drinking was really about part of me longing to feel less awkward. In my twenties (when I was partying hard), drinking was really about part of me longing to feel less responsible. In my thirties (when I was living with domestic violence), drinking was really about part of me longing to feel less trapped. In my early forties (as a busy working parent), drinking was really about part of me longing to feel less stressed out. At the height of the pandemic (as a business owner and a home-school teacher to my kids), drinking was really about part of me longing to feel less overwhelmed.

Don't get me wrong, I am no angel. I still have the occasional drink, and I don't always drink purely for the enjoyment of it. The difference is that, today, I have much more awareness of the inner dialogue behind my decision to open a bottle of wine. I experience more choice and agency in how I care for myself.

Here are a few common examples of Distractor Parts:

The Snack Monster Part

A part whose job it is to convince you that chocolate would make life so much better right now. This part will also find any excuse to celebrate, relax or treat themself to something sweet or salty (or both in the case of my Sea-salt-dark-chocolate Craving Part). What this part really wants is to feel less of the hard stuff for a blissful few sweet or salty moments.

The Shop-a-holic Part

A part who just can't resist the temptation of buying something new and shiny to momentarily feel better about themself. This part may shop in a way that feels almost compulsive, propelled by the misguided hope that if we have enough nice stuff, then we will one day feel like we are enough. Often, this part experiences buyer's remorse, or may even try to hide new purchases from loved ones ('This old thing? No, it's not new, I've had it for ages!'). After-pay companies love this part.

The Work-a-holic Part

A part that really struggles to switch off from work, even though deep down you know that what you're working on late at night is neither important nor urgent. This part just can't seem to stop. They work hard in a way that goes beyond healthy striving or putting in extra time to meet the occasional deadline. They keep you stuck in habitual patterns of working long hours yet never feeling 'on top' of things. They're great at justifying their over-working through excuses of being 'busy and important', but deep down they feel powerless to stop because they're desperate to distract us from opening the can of worms that is the buried feelings of our most vulnerable parts.

It's important to mention here that we all numb ourselves in one way or another. Life can be incredibly challenging, and sometimes we just need to do something that feels soothing or distracting. There is nothing inherently 'wrong' or 'bad' about having Distractor Parts. We all have them.

However, challenges arise when these parts pull us into destructive or addictive patterns and when the costs of their distraction strategies become problematic for us or for the people we love. When Distractor Parts do their thing to 'take the edge off' our fear, overwhelm, frustration, loneliness or sadness, they also dull feelings of connection, love, gratitude and joy.

By getting to know our Distractor Parts, we can better understand what they are afraid would happen if they did not do what they do. From there, we can begin the gentle process of witnessing, caring for and, ultimately (with the right support), dissolving the heavy burdens carried by the Injured Parts they are protecting.

Over time, we can cultivate greater confidence in our capacity to care for the most vulnerable parts of ourselves in the way they need to be cared for. This means that our Distractor Parts have less need to take drastic action and are activated less and less frequently.

HOW PARTS ALTER THE EXPRESSION OF OUR ESSENTIAL NATURE

While all our parts have good intentions, they are often misguided in the best way to keep us safe and connected. Our parts don't always accurately reflect our true nature and our innate leadership qualities. Sometimes, parts can alter the expression of our best qualities, causing this expression to be extreme, exaggerated or distorted.

Here are just a few examples of the ways parts can alter the expression of your essence:

- A part that feels driven to prove itself can mutate natural confidence into arrogance.
- A part that feels like an outsider might distort our capacity to maintain a healthy sense of independence into more extreme 'lone wolf' behaviours.
- A part that believes that things need to be perfect might impede access to our creativity.
- A part that is terrified of looking silly, childish or naïve might restrict access to our playfulness.
- A part that holds impossibly high standards might block our natural compassion (for ourselves and others).
- A part that feels the urge to fight for justice might corrupt our courage into a more aggressive, perhaps combative energy.
- A part that is petrified of not being needed can taint our natural inclination to be of service, distorting it into an unhealthy need to always be involved.

Exploring uncharted territory

Being true is a pilgrimage of discovery. There are no clear pathways to follow because you are exploring uncharted territory. These practices will call you to venture beyond your current boundaries, each next best action revealing itself as you move forward and respond to what you encounter.

Matt Licata writes, 'There is a map written inside you in a language that only you can decipher.'[49] Creating and evolving a map of your inner world is best approached with curiosity and patience. Only by showing your parts that you have no ulterior motive and genuinely want to understand them will you move towards greater inner harmony. I encourage you to take your time with all the practices you will learn in the second section of the book.

All your parts will respond to being compassionately witnessed, welcomed and, over time, appreciated by you. No matter how elaborate or unusual the map of your inner system, it will make perfect sense to you. You are the only person who can illuminate and observe the one-of-a-kind inhabitants who occupy your one-of-a-kind inner world, assisted or unassisted. Seeking the guidance and support of an IFS-trained coach or therapist may be helpful, but it is not essential.

The only exception is if you want to work more deeply with your 'exiled' Injured Parts. To do this deeper work safely, it is advisable to seek the support of a trained IFS therapist. Your Injured Parts carry traumas from your past. Expert guidance is required to ensure that you are not overwhelmed by the feelings associated with these past events. I have personally worked through the experience of unburdening my exiles with my IFS therapist, and have benefited enormously. You will find details on the IFS Institute website in the Resources section of this book. Here you will find a directory of IFS therapists.

PRINCIPLE 5:

Being true to yourself takes playful practice

When we play, we are engaged in the purest expression of our humanity, the truest expression of our individuality. The road to mastery of any subject is guided by play.

DR STUART BROWN

During my corporate leadership career, I worked for an exceptional leader. Naomi was smart and kind, savvy and playful, commercially minded and warm-hearted. My fondest memory of our time working together was the morning when I rushed into her office, heavily pregnant and in a mild state of panic. I had just been informed at my routine ultrasound appointment that the size of my soon-to-be-born son's head circumference was in the ninety-fifth percentile. Given my height is somewhere around the fifth percentile, this news had conjured up all sorts of gruesome images in my hormone-soaked mind of my lady-bits tearing. After several unsuccessful attempts at reassuring me that it would all be fine, she leaped to her feet, grabbed a marker and drew two circles on her whiteboard – one a tiny fraction bigger than the other. Pointing to one circle, then the next, she said, 'Cassie, you are talking about the difference between this and this. Either way, it's gonna hurt like hell.'

The reason I loved Naomi so much in that moment – and in so many other similar shared moments of laughter (and tears) over the years we worked together – is that she was so real. When it came to great leadership, she was the real deal, and she was a natural.

On another occasion, I was in Naomi's office lamenting the latest 'schoolyard antics' of some of the senior leaders in our organisation and the havoc their shenanigans were creating for my project time-lines. After patiently hearing me out, Naomi said something that has always stayed with me. She said, 'Cassie, try thinking about all of this as a big game. Try something, and if it doesn't work, try something different. Just keep on playing.'

We are conditioned to believe that work is the opposite of play – but this is a lie. The opposite of play is depression.[50] As humans, we are designed to flourish through play. Play is essential to our social skills, adaptability, intelligence, creativity and the ability to learn and solve problems. There is indisputable evidence that play is a fundamental human biological drive and is just as essential to our ability to thrive as sleep or nutrition.[51] And in tough times, we need to play more than ever.

Dr Charles Schaefer is the father of play therapy. He said, 'We are never more fully alive, more completely ourselves than when we are playing.' Sadly, Dr Schaefer passed away suddenly in late 2020. His obituary describes him as a person who was: 'Profoundly gentle, unfailingly kind, deeply thoughtful, and always funny.' When it comes to great ways to be remembered, these nine words are hard to beat.

So, what does it mean to bring our innate playfulness to the practice of being true? Let's first take a closer look at what it means to practise.

A practice is something you intentionally engage in to experience some sort of benefit. You can practise yoga to reconnect to your body. You can practise meditation to become more mindfully aware of your thoughts and feelings without identifying with them.

The practices you will learn in *Being True* will empower and enable you to connect with your essential nature, and to take good care of your many different parts. The more you practise, the more skilled you will become at acknowledging and confidently working with your parts with curiosity and compassion. I encourage you to bring a sense of lightness and play to your practices of *Being True*.

Try to approach all interactions with your parts in the same spirit of tender-hearted, joyful curiosity someone might experience when they surrender to playing on the floor with their toddler or beloved pet. Whether or not you are a parent or a pet-lover, we can all choose to embody our innate, playful nature.

The other point worth mentioning here is that practice requires commitment. We all love the idea of a quick fix, and there are plenty of other books that will promise you one. However, the truth is that there are no ten easy-to-follow steps when it comes to the work of being true to ourselves. That would be too simplistic to be effective. We are complex living systems living within complex living systems.

You will not experience the full benefits of the practices in *Being True* if you try things only once or wait until the weekend or your next holiday to start. You will get the best results through daily playful practice. Being true requires sustained commitment and ongoing moment-to-moment awareness.

So, the bad news is that there is no finish line you sprint across. But the good news is that it is not time-consuming or hard to practise. The concepts and the practices you will learn in this next section of the book can be practised in the flow of your everyday working life.

My suggestion is that you read through all five practices, let them all marinate a little and then circle back and pick just one thing you feel you can commit to putting into regular practice. Then play with this one practice as often as you can for around six to eight weeks. Once this first practice feels like it has become habitual, you can determine the next best practice to begin playing with.

There really is no rush. You'll get the best results if you enjoy the process. Remember, feeling free to be more yourself flows from your sustained commitment to playful practice, so do your best to hold things lightly and be kind to yourself.

PRACTICES

We are not trying to change ourselves;
we're not trying to fix anything.
Rather, we get curious about who we are,
how our mind works.
We practice to remove obstacles
that cover up our basic goodness,
the fine qualities of being
that humans never lose.

MARGARET J. WHEATLEY[52]

OVERVIEW OF THE FIVE PRACTICES

Here is an overview of the five practices we'll be playing with in this next section.

Discovering your inner team	You'll practise staying in the driver's seat instead of being swept away by your inner dialogue. The intention of this practice is to create a sense of inner spaciousness so you can begin to relate to your parts from a place of connection to the qualities of your core self.
Understanding the key players	You'll be guided to get curious about the many different aspects of yourself. The intention of this practice is to become more familiar with the key players and the dynamics of your inner world.
Caring for your parts	You'll be supported to extend compassionate reassurance to the parts of you that need your leadership. The intention of this practice is to build on your understanding of your parts to care for them in very specific ways and create your inner alliance.
Remembering who you are	You'll reignite vital aspects of yourself that have been turned down to pilot-light setting. The intention of this practice is to salvage vital aspects of yourself that you have forgotten, lost connection with or abandoned.
Harnessing your essence	You'll play with connecting to your essence as an uplifting and renewable energy source. The intention of this practice is to tap into a powerful, inner source of energy and vitality that has the potential to uplift you, those you lead and those you love.

PRACTICE 1:

Discovering your inner team

*When I honour my multidimensionality, I
am freed to acknowledge and honour all the
parts of me. I get space to breathe.*
JENNA REIMERSMA[53]

The first practice we're going to play with is the practice of discovering your inner team of parts. The intention of this practice is to open up a little bit of space between you and your parts, so that you can begin to relate to your parts with a strong connection to the qualities of your core self. This powerful foundational practice shifts your perspective from *being* your parts to *seeing* your parts.

WHY PRACTISE?

To practise self-coaching, self-care or self-leadership, you first need to open up some space inside of you. To do this, you must first discover the part that has been activated, and then create some space between your part and your core self. You can do this through what can be described as 'unblending'.

Scott, a client I worked with, once shared his frustration that he was great at coaching his direct reports, but rubbish at coaching himself. Scott was unsure as to why that was. After I taught Scott the practice of discovering and unblending from his parts, he became much more confident in his capacity to coach himself.

Until we learn how to discover and unblend from our parts, it is impossible to coach ourselves. We have all experienced moments when we find ourselves behaving in ways that are way out of alignment with who we really are. In these moments it can feel like we have been hijacked by a mysterious force that's out of our control.

Over my career, I have often had flashbacks of a famous scene from *The Wizard of Oz*. The one towards the end, where the curtain is pulled back to reveal the hidden workings of the almighty Oz, who is really a frightened, sweaty little man frantically pulling levers.

In moments when we behave in ways we don't feel proud of, it's because another part of ourselves has taken over the controls. When we are blended with a part, the thoughts, emotions and urges of the part become our own. But there is a way out *if* we can remember that our thoughts emanate from our parts. The good news is that we can practise unblending from our parts to regain access to a wiser, calmer and more resourced version of ourselves. Unblending from our parts opens up space inside of us to relate to our parts from more solid ground – a connection to our core self.

As Viktor E. Frankl explained, 'Between stimulus and response there is a space. In that space is our power to choose our response. In our

response lies our growth and our freedom.' Discovering and sepa-
rating from our parts opens space within us. This space allows us to
become aware of our parts and opens the possibility of responding
more skilfully and truthfully to the world around us, rather than
blindly reacting.

The main goal is to practise seeing your parts and letting your parts
know that you see them. As you unblend from your parts, you naturally regain access to the powerful qualities of your core self, and
you dial down the intensity of the emotional contagion happening
between your parts and you.

In the past, I have been hijacked by a younger, vulnerable part at
the family dinner table. As much as it pains me to admit this, I have
been known to spend family dinners completely withdrawn and
lost in my inner world, utterly convinced of my aloneness while
being surrounded by the people I love most. By getting curious
about these hijackings, I came to realise that they were triggered by
something very specific. This trigger was something that happened
before dinner, or rather something that did *not* happen. I realised
that my withdrawn part was activated by my husband failing to ask
me how my day was within the first few minutes of arriving home.
The absence of this simple, timely question from my husband was
enough to activate this part, which I realised attached her self-worth
to recognition. I now call her 'Little Miss Achiever'. For her, achievements serve one purpose and one purpose only – currency to be
exchanged for proof of her enough-ness. Without this exchange
(my achievements traded for my next 'gold star'), this part of me
felt worthless – and, worse still, she felt like all her hard work was

a complete waste of effort. So, even after a great day when I had achieved great things, if these achievements were not recognised by my husband, I could become consumed by feelings of emptiness, worthlessness and hopelessness. Discovering this part, and the tell-tale signs she had been activated (feeling alone and resentful towards my poor husband), was the first step towards more inner peace and more grown-up behaviours at the dinner table!

Today, I am rarely hijacked by Little Miss Achiever. I have figured out the best ways to check in with her at the end of my working day. I might take a few minutes on my drive home to tell her that she has done great today and to remind her that she is loved, and she is worthy – just because of who she is. When I remember to do this end-of-day ritual, I find myself looking forward to asking my husband and my kids about their days rather than anxiously hoping that someone will validate my worthiness by asking about mine.

To have any chance of unblending from an activated part, you must be able to recall that your thoughts are simply reactive, habitual (often disempowered) patterns. This is tricky. Most of the time you'll completely forget this. This is totally normal. Most of us spend most of our days completely consumed by our thoughts and blended with our many parts. The good news is that the more you practise remembering, discovering and unblending, the better you'll get at it.

HOW TO PRACTISE

The practice of discovering an activated part is not complicated. However, our minds are slippery little suckers and can be hard to catch. If we can remember that we have many parts, the actual practice of unblending is very straightforward.

Moments when you notice that you are feeling frustrated, angry, afraid, anxious or overwhelmed are great moments to practise. It may be easiest to notice these sensations first in your body, perhaps in the form of tightness in your shoulders, gripping at the back of your eyes or clenching your jaw. If we are listening, our body sends us many signals that a part has become activated. The quality that is most helpful to stay tethered to as you practise discovering your parts is your curiosity. Try to approach your journey of inner discovery in the spirit of curiosity – with a genuine desire to get to know yourself better. Intentionally harnessing your innate curiosity enables other qualities of your essential nature to assist you, such as your compassion, playfulness, creativity and patience. You can practise parts discovery in the moment when a part of you has been activated, or retrospectively in the hours or days after.

In-the-moment parts discovery becomes possible if (and that's a big 'if') you catch yourself being swept away in the drama of a part's narrative. This is tricky and often beyond our reach in moments of heightened emotions. Forgetting about the whole concept of parts in the heat of the moment is completely normal. Please be sure to remind your inner-judge parts of this when they try to give you a hard time about it.

The opportunity for a retrospective practice arises when you notice yourself replaying a scene over and over in your head or ruminating on all the things you should have said or done differently. In this situation, you can take a few moments to get still and quiet and try the parts discovery practice.

The crux of the practice is speaking *for* your part, instead of *from* your part. One of the easiest ways to do this is to use this prompt: 'Part of me...'

For example, if you suddenly feel convinced that you can't handle a particular situation, you can identify and unblend from your activated part by thinking or saying: 'Part of me feels totally overwhelmed right now.' The difference between silently saying to yourself, 'Part of me feels totally overwhelmed right now,' and being engulfed by the thought, 'I can't handle this,' may be subtle, but it's also very powerful. As you practise, pay attention to what this shift in perspective does inside you. You might notice it has a calming effect on your body and mind, or things might feel lighter, more hopeful or a little less 'personal'.

Another entry point to parts discovery is to ask yourself, 'What part of me is struggling with this?' or 'What part of me is feeling resentful right now?' (Or hesitant, afraid, unsure, sad, frustrated, anxious and other feelings.)

Once you have discovered an activated part and remembered to say to yourself some version of: 'Part of me feels totally overwhelmed right now,' then you can open more space inside by asking your part a few questions. It might sound strange at first, but in the same way you might speak to a scared or lost child, you could ask your activated part if there is anything it wants you to know, or anything that it needs from you. We will further explore this in subsequent practices.

Our parts want to communicate with us, and what they reveal can be surprising. When engaging with a part, don't expect to hear an actual voice that speaks back to you. Your parts will most likely communicate with you through symbols, images, memories, feelings and impressions of thoughts.

LET'S PRACTISE

To practise discovering your inner team of parts, you can ask yourself these questions:

- What's coming up for me right now?
- What part or parts of me are struggling with this?
- What am I feeling right now, and which part of me feels it?

Or you can complete this statement:

Part of me is feeling _____ and another part of me is feeling _____, but deep down I know _____.

Understanding the key players

True personal growth is about transcending the part of you that is not okay and needs protection. This is done by constantly remembering that you are the one inside that notices the voice talking. That is the way out.

MICHAEL A. SINGER

The next practice I invite you to play with is the practice of understanding the key players in your inner team. The intention of this practice is to become more familiar with the dynamics of your inner world. Understanding your different parts and learning how to relate to them from this place of calm understanding is an essential life skill, and it's arguably the most important leadership capability that exists.

WHY PRACTISE?

As we have learned, inside every person exists a unique and elaborate system of parts with a uniting core self. And, as you're hopefully beginning to discover, it's possible to access your inner world and nurture healthy relationships with your different parts. This next practice is all about getting curious about your parts – with a genuine desire to understand them.

The practice of understanding your parts becomes easier and more enjoyable if you can open your mind to the possibility that your parts are like little beings that dwell inside you. I love how Dr Richard Schwartz describes parts:[54]

'They're little inner beings that are trying their best to keep you safe and to keep each other safe and to keep it together in there. They have full-range personalities: each of them has different desires, different ages, different opinions, different talents, and different resources. Instead of just being annoyances or afflictions (which they can be in their extreme roles) they are wonderful inner beings.'

Remember, the colourful characters you encounter in this inner world may not be what they seem. By trusting that none of your parts is bad and that they are all doing their best to keep you feeling safe, connected and worthy, it becomes possible to get to know them.

For a brief period in my early twenties, I had a second job working as a DJ for a mobile party company. My job required me to travel to eighteenth and twenty-first birthday parties at RSL clubs across Sydney. My uniform consisted of black slacks, a white-collared shirt, a thick red satin cummerbund and matching red bowtie. I sucked at being a DJ. I shook with nerves every time I had to make an announcement on the microphone and spent most of the night standing stiffly behind my decks.

To get through each excruciating party, I devised a standard playlist. I would always play *Girls Just Want To Have Fun* by Cyndi Lauper (a cry for help), *Love Shack* by the B-52s (because it was the 90s) and *American Pie* by Don McLean (because it was over eight minutes long, giving me enough time to go to the toilet). I decided to hang up my red bowtie for good when, after walking into an RSL club one Saturday evening to set up, with my huge bank of flashing lights under my arm, a wide-eyed young partygoer elbowed his mate and loudly exclaimed, 'Awesome! They've hired a stripper!'

Much like I did during my short-lived stint as a DJ, your parts have a limited and predictable playlist. We can't turn our parts off, but through practice and patience, we can learn how to turn down the volume on their thoughts and impulses.

Often, when I support my clients to begin to engage with the different parts of themselves, they can experience some level of trepidation. This is usually because a Protector Part whispers some version of this warning: 'Don't start meddling around inside; it's scary and risky. You're barely holding it together as it is – don't rock the boat.' It's important to acknowledge these concerns while also not letting these fears prevent you from taking gentle steps towards getting to know your parts. Proceed carefully and respectfully, seeking per-mission to proceed every step of the way. The point here is simply to get to know the inhabitants of your inner world, not to change them or judge them. Your parts are your inner heroes and showing them how much you appreciate them is essential throughout your self-discovery journey, but especially in these early stages.

In Principle 4: *You have a core and many parts*, I shared some detailed examples of different types of parts. Getting to know your Protector Parts is a good place to begin the practice of understanding your parts. To help give you a sense for what you may encounter, here are some further examples of different Protector Parts and their life mottos.

Judgemental Part:	To survive, you've got to figure out what's wrong.
Controlling Part:	You've got to stay in control, whatever it takes.
Hyper Achiever Part:	Your achievements are proof of your worthiness.
Catastrophising Part:	It is going to be this bad forever and life will be unbearable.
Victimised Part:	The deck is stacked against you, and you are powerless.
Know-It-All Part:	You should have all the answers.
Hyper Planner Part:	You must have a plan for every possible scenario.
People Pleaser Part:	You should always put the needs of others first.
Pusher Part:	You should be working harder – it's not enough.
Comparer Part:	You are so much better/worse than that person.
Impossible Standards Setter Part:	It has to be perfect – you've got to get it right.
Mr Tough Guy Part:	Whatever happens, don't show any sign of weakness.

Fixed Mindset Part:	You'll never get it.
Discomfort Avoider Part:	Don't even try – you won't be able to handle it.
Just Lucky Part:	You just got lucky this one time.
Imposter Part:	You are a total fraud – and any day now they'll find you out.
Shamer Part:	You'll never be good enough – there's something wrong with you.
Critical Part:	You're stupid/weak/naïve/selfish/ ugly/fat/greedy/disgusting.
Fear of Failure Part:	You're just going to make a complete fool of yourself.
Wine Lover Part:	Just have a drink – you'll feel better. You deserve it.
Shop-a-holic Part:	Buy something nice and just forget about everything for a while.

HOW TO PRACTISE

This practice has been inspired by and adapted from the work of Dr Richard Schwartz and the training I have completed with the IFS Institute.[55]

This practice takes the form of a guided experience of self-inquiry.

I recommend having a journal or something to capture notes as you practise.

You may find it helpful to create your own map or representation of your inner system to orient yourself as you explore within. As new parts emerge, you can add them to your map, and as you get better at recognising your loudest inner residents, you can get better at welcoming them back and gaining their trust.

It's not critical to figure out whether your parts are Manager Parts, Distractor Parts or Injured Parts. Just focus on beginning to capture them in a form that makes sense to you. When I run in-person workshops, some participants love bringing their most familiar parts to life by decorating plain wooden babushka doll sets. If this sounds like something you might enjoy, you'll find these sets in craft stores. Your emerging Inner Alliance Map (or babushka doll set) will be messy, incomplete and unique, but it will make perfect sense to you. Remember that it's a perpetual work-in-progress.

Engaging in an inner dialogue with your parts can be surprisingly revealing. They have important messages to share with you. When approached with creativity and playfulness, along with an open heart and an open mind, you may discover that the inhabitants of your inner world are quite eager to introduce themselves to you and begin to tell their stories.

Try not to be too discouraged if at first you don't get any new insights. Sometimes, we must gently peel back the layers of ourselves to open the lines of communication. We can do this through the initial steps in the practice and by sending our parts messages of reassurance that there is space for all of them.

LET'S PRACTISE

To begin, get comfortable and come back to your senses. Simply rest your attention on one of your senses for three to five breaths.

What can you see, feel, taste, smell or hear?

The next step is to do a scan of your body with the intention of noticing any thoughts, emotions, sensations or impulses that are present for you. Just notice what's there.

Now, sense whether there is anything that seems to want your attention. It could be a particular thought, emotion, sensation or impulse that seems to be calling out to you.

Just sense if there is something within you that you'd like to get to know better.

Once you have identified a particular thought, emotion, sensation or impulse to work with, focus on it for a minute or two. Just let whatever is there be there.

Next, if you can, try to sense where this part is in your body. As you do that, just notice if there are any thoughts, words or images that come to you. Continue patiently and quietly observe what's arising.

When it feels right to do so, pause and capture whatever you have noticed.

Once you have drawn, written or sketched whatever has arisen, take a few moments to ask the following questions: What is this part saying to me? Is there more?

Make a note of anything further that comes up.

As you're taking all of this in, see if you can also notice how you are feeling *towards* this part of you. Do you wish they would go away? Do they annoy or frustrate you? Do you feel dependent on them somehow? Do you resent them? Are you somehow afraid of them?

If you're not feeling some level of openness or curiosity towards the target part, it just means that there are other parts activated. If this is the case, try gently asking these parts of you to step back, and respectfully request a little space to get to know the part you have chosen to focus on a little better.

If you can sense openness and curiosity towards the part, you can begin to interact with them by asking some questions. Try not to predict the answers. Instead, rest your attention on the part of your body where you sense the part is located and wait. Don't worry if you can't hear any clear answers, just try to sense a response. Be still and quiet and wait to see if an answer arises – if not, that's completely okay.

Ask the part if it is okay to ask a few questions.

If you sense they are open, then you can try asking some (or all) of the following questions:

- What is your role or purpose?
- How long have you been doing this for me?
- What was happening in my life when you first started doing this?
- What is your highest intention for me?
- How old are you?
- How old do you think I am?
- How do you feel about your role today?
- Is there anything else you want me to know?

To close the practice, extend your appreciation to all your parts, for the jobs they do and for doing their best to keep you safe and connected.

Finally, don't forget to jot down anything you wish to remember and come back to.

PRACTICE 3:

Caring for your parts

*Once we take the inner realm seriously, respecting
its inhabitants and their laws, we learn that
the psyche has the wisdom to heal itself.*
DR RICHARD SCHWARTZ[56]

In the next practice I invite you to begin the practice of caring for your parts. The intention of this practice is to build on your understanding of your parts to care for them.

You'll soon discover that each of your parts needs to be cared for in very specific ways. And you are the only person who can care for your parts in the way they need to be cared for. This is because you are the only person who understands what they have been through.

WHY PRACTISE?

Through understanding our parts, we naturally begin to feel compassion and care towards them. As we find the courage to care for our parts, we naturally begin to relate in a healing way to ourselves and to other people.

The extent to which we can access the qualities of our core self depends on the extent to which we understand the hurts, fears and needs of our parts – and how well we take care of them. By learning how to take good care of our parts, we reduce the likelihood that our parts will sabotage us out of fear or desperation.

Over time, through committed, compassionate practice, our inner relationships deepen and we become the trusted leader of our parts. As our parts experience our care and begin to trust that things go better when we're in charge, they can become our greatest supporters – a united inner team of advisers. An inner alliance.

As you are discovering, each of your parts has their own unique world view and corresponding pattern of thinking and behaving. Our parts all come into existence because they believe that there is an important job that needs doing – and that they have no choice but to take on this job. They truly are our inner everyday heroes.

Remember, your parts want to keep you safe, protected and connected. The problem is, because of past injuries, your parts can carry misguided beliefs about why you have not been cared for in the past – and what it will require to become worthy of love and care.

As you get to know your parts, you may come to see that they don't necessarily enjoy their jobs or want to keep doing them, but they feel they have no choice. They may need your help to retire from their self-appointed, exhausting jobs and find more empowered roles to play in your inner system. Roles that require less vigilance and help move your whole inner system towards harmony.

The beliefs and fears your parts carry are formed in childhood moments – perhaps in moments when you did not feel loved and cared for. Because it would be too terrifying for your young mind to consider that the grown-ups made mistakes, you very naturally concluded that you were somehow the problem. That you had to be more or less of something to be worthy of love. And so, your parts came to believe that there were certain conditions that you must meet to be worthy of love and belonging. Because your parts took on these burdens when you were so young, they became frozen in that time. They may believe that you are still very young, perhaps three, five or seven years old.

When you were a small child, your survival really did depend on not being rejected by your family or caregivers. This explains why, in moments when a part of you believes that you have fallen short of their criteria, you may feel you are in a life-or-death situation.

I once guided a client called Mary through her first encounter with a younger part of her. This part of Mary had been working away for over five decades outside her conscious awareness. Mary sensed that this part was probably around five years old. They were convinced that no one was paying attention to them, and that nobody cared about them. They felt all alone in the world. I was able to guide Mary to have a conversation with her five-year-old part. Through this conversation, Mary was able to help the part to realise (much to their surprise) that Mary was now a fully grown woman, and, most importantly, that they were not alone – Mary was there to care for them in the way they needed to be cared for. This process of 'updating' the part about Mary's current age and the reassurance of discovering there was a grown-up who wanted to care for them had a significant, positive impact for Mary.

It took less than thirty minutes of gentle, guided dialogue with her five-year-old part, seeking permission every step of the way, to begin the process of dissolving the heavy burdens this part had been carrying for so long. Mary reported experiencing a deep sense of relief following this brief interaction with her part.

Here are just a few examples of the criteria for enough-ness that our parts can become burdened with, beginning with the prompt: 'To be enough, to be safe and to survive I must...'

- Be the smartest person in the room
- Always look like I know the answer
- Always have a plan
- Always be immaculately groomed
- Be thin and attractive
- Always anticipate what's about to happen
- Always be included
- Always be in control
- Never show any sign of weakness

Because of experiences I had in my formative years when my feelings sometimes felt dangerous, part of me decided that I needed to transform myself into a high-achieving-low-maintenance machine to be worthy of love and belonging. You guessed it, this was the birth of Little Miss Achiever and her life motto of 'never enough'. Little Miss Achiever will always be part of me, but today she is rarely in the driver's seat. Today, I understand that she is too young to even hold a driver's licence. I appreciate her for doing her part to keep the peace when I was little, for propelling my early career success and for inspiring the work I do today, but I know that her paradigm puts me at very real risk of burnout.

I know that I am not alone in having a relentlessly striving, high-achieving part driven by the belief that she will one day achieve her way to worthiness. Many high-flying leaders live with a part that measures their value in the world only through the currency of achievements, accolades and status. All too often, low self-worth is the shadow-side of high performance.

As we de-couple our sense of self-worth from external measures of success and learn to draw on the power of our essence as an alternative energy source, our performance becomes sustainable, we work better with others and we feel more uplifted and alive. More on this later.

Pema Chödrön said, 'When we protect ourselves so we won't feel pain, that protection becomes armour, like armour that imprisons the softness of the heart.' A coaching client recently realised that while she thought she needed to learn how to protect herself more at work (to get through an impending restructure), what she really needed was to learn how to **care** for the most vulnerable parts of herself.

The working world can condition us to think that we need to shield our hearts – over time, this way of thinking forms a belief. We come to believe that we must shield our hearts to protect ourselves from the slings and arrows of the world. As we all know, unfortunately, these slings and arrows can be particularly prevalent and cutting in our workplaces. The challenge is that by permanently shielding our hearts, we cut ourselves off from the care and connection we are so desperately longing for.

The first step to releasing the burden of the belief that we must shield our hearts is to be aware of its existence. From this place of awareness, we can begin to find the courage to lay down our heavy armour and to learn how to care for ourselves, so we feel resourced enough to keep our hearts more open, despite the risk of heartbreak.

Another point worth noting here is that, just like our children, our parts need our care *most* when they *least* deserve it. Because we have been conditioned to believe that children who 'misbehave' must be punished, this may be challenging. However, it's when inner voices are loud and mean, or when your urges and compulsions are strongest, that your parts are most in need of your care.

As we have learned, no two parts are the same. In the same way I have learned that my two young sons each respond very differently when they hurt themselves, different parts need different things from us. With practice you'll discover the best way to care for and reassure your parts. To begin, the goal is simply to open a line of communication with your parts, to reassure them that they are not alone in there.

The practice of caring for your parts is something that you can call on throughout your working day. I am going to share two different ways you can do this through parts reassurance and parts dialogue.

HOW TO PRACTISE

Parts reassurance
The next time you sense inner frustration, anxiety, sadness, resentment, fear or judgement, you can silently send compassionate reassurance to your activated part or parts.

It may be helpful to reflect on what you needed to hear from your parents or caregivers when you were upset or afraid as a child. You may even like to imagine your five-year-old self there with you and to practise saying the words your younger self most needed to hear from a grown-up.

I encourage you to play with different messages of reassurance to get a felt sense for how your parts respond to these messages. Over time, trust that you can figure out precisely what your part most needs to hear from you in difficult moments. You are the best person to care for and reassure your parts in the way they need to be cared for and reassured, because you are the only person in the world who really understands the burdens they've been carrying for so long.

LET'S PRACTISE

To practise reassuring your parts, start by taking a few deep breaths.

Next, imagine your younger self, or focus your attention on any physical sensations you are experiencing.

Then, silently send your caring reassurance to the activated part or parts, for example:

- I see you – you matter.
- There's space for you here too.
- I love you, and I am listening.
- Just try to relax a little.
- I'm here for you.
- I can see that this is hard for you.
- We're going to get through this.
- You are not alone.
- It's going to be okay.
- This is not about you.

HOW TO PRACTISE

Parts dialogue

Another way to practise caring for your parts is to engage in dialogue with them. This practice builds on the guided practice you learned in Practice 2: *Understanding the key players*. The first part of the practice is similar, but the questions are a little different. You will be guided to focus on building on your current understanding of the part to get a deeper sense of the inner dynamic at play.

This practice may begin to illuminate the Injured Parts that your Protector Parts are working hard to keep locked away. As I suggested in the introduction, please seek the support of a trained IFS therapist if you feel it would be beneficial to begin working more directly with your Injured Parts.

LET'S PRACTISE

Begin by coming back to your senses. Focus your attention on one of your senses for three to five breaths.

What can you see, feel, taste, smell or hear?

The next step is to do a scan of your body with the intention of noticing any thoughts, emotions, sensations or impulses that are present for you.

Now, sense whether there is anything that seems to want your attention: a thought, emotion, sensation or impulse that seems to be calling to you or speaking to you most loudly. Sense if there is something within you that you'd like to know better.

Once you have identified a particular thought, emotion, sensation or impulse to work with, focus on it for a minute or two, just letting whatever is there be there.

Next, if you can, try to sense where this part is in your body. As you do that, just notice if there are any thoughts, words or images that come to you.

Continue patiently and quietly observing what arises.

As you are taking all of this in, see if you can also notice how you are feeling *towards* this part of you. Do you wish they would go away? Do they annoy or frustrate you? Do you feel dependent on them somehow? Do you resent them? Are you somehow afraid of them?

If you are not feeling some level of openness or curiosity towards the target part, it just means that there are other parts activated. If this is the case, try gently asking these parts of you to step back, and respectfully request a little space to get to know the part you have chosen to focus on a little better.

If you can sense openness and curiosity towards the part, you can begin to interact with them by asking some questions. Try not to predict the answers. Instead, rest your attention on the part of your body where you sense the part is located and wait. Don't worry if you can't 'hear' any clear answers, just try to sense a response. Be still and quiet and wait to see if an answer arises – if not, that's completely okay.

Start by asking the part if it is okay to ask them a few questions. If you sense they are open, you can try asking some (or all) of the following questions:

- What is your role or purpose? (You may already have a sense for this.)
- What are you afraid might happen if you do not do this?
- What can I do to help?
- Is there anything else you want me to know?

To close the practice, extend your appreciation to all your parts for the important jobs they do and for doing their best to keep you safe and connected.

Finally, don't forget to jot down anything you wish to remember and come back to.

Remembering who you are

You are the sky. Everything else – it's just the weather.
PEMA CHÖDRÖN

This next practice we're going to play with is the practice of remembering who you are at your core, and reconnecting to the powerful and enduring qualities of your true nature. The intention of this practice is to salvage vital aspects of yourself that you have forgotten, lost connection with or abandoned.

WHY PRACTISE?

There can be lots of reasons why we lose connection with certain aspects of ourselves. When we feel inadequate, inappropriate or inconvenient, overwhelming feelings can cause us to lock parts of ourselves away. As we have learned, sometimes vital aspects of our true nature have been exiled with our Injured Parts.

Sometimes, the experiences that sever our connection with our core happen in our formative years. I don't have many memories of my childhood, but I do have a strong recollection of the day I wrote a poem about the miracle of an egg becoming a chick. I was probably around eight years old. I distinctly remember my face burning with shame at the front of the classroom as my teacher looked up from reading the poem I had carefully written in my very best writing. My memory is of her looking down at me with a look of disdain, and saying in a tone of exacerbation, 'Cassie, it's just an egg!' Because I was a highly conscientious little girl who really relied on my teacher to validate my enough-ness, this moment was particularly crushing. It felt so deeply humiliating that it encoded a belief into my young brain that to write and wonder about things that could not be easily explained or understood was both dangerous and naïve. It took until my late thirties to became aware of and let go of this limiting belief. If I were still unknowingly burdened by that belief, this book would not exist.

Experiences that weaken our connection to our true nature can also happen in our adult lives. Many years ago, I had a manager who told me in my annual performance review: 'The problem with you, Cassie, is that you care too much. If you want to progress to an executive position, you must learn to care less.' He did not deliver this feedback in a patronising or mean way. He genuinely felt he was sharing his secret to success with me. However, I knew that, for me, trying to care less about the work I do and the people I do it with would be like trying to hold a beachball under water for forty hours each week. I was able to respectfully deflect this well-meaning but ill-informed advice and went on to become a deeply caring and high-performing global executive.

Forgetting, suppressing, disowning or abandoning any element of our essential nature for extended periods of time makes us sick, sad and lonely.

Unfortunately, the leaders I coach often tell me that they feel disconnected from their creativity, playfulness, patience, presence, compassion or vitality. Often, these leaders have come to believe unhelpful falsehoods about these innate qualities.

I have had heard leaders say things like:

- Only some people are creative – and I'm just not one of them.
- Being playful is never appropriate at my workplace.
- Being playful is childish.
- I'm just not someone who is compassionate.
- I'm just too busy to be fully present – I am constantly multitasking; it's the only way I can keep on top of things.
- I am totally disconnected from my body.
- I just don't have time to take care of myself.

To recap, our shared essential nature is a way of describing the indestructible core of goodness inside each one of us. It's the home of our most positively powerful leadership attributes. It's the truth of who we *really* are beneath all the protective, defensive layers we have accumulated over the years. It's the real person beneath our personality.

HOW TO PRACTISE

There are three interwoven aspects to the practice of reconnecting to your true nature: Letting Go, Letting In and Letting Be. This language comes from the work of Dr Rick Hanson.[57] These practices take the form of reflective self-inquiry. I recommend having a journal or something you can capture notes on at hand.

Here is a brief explanation of these three aspects:

- **Letting Go:** Releasing the things that disempower you.
- **Letting In:** Firing up your life-force.
- **Letting Be**: Allowing the expression of your true nature.

How might life be different if you trusted deeply that everything you need to be an inspiring leader is already inside you? What would it mean to have an unshakable faith that the wisest, calmest, most patient and compassionate version of you is your true identity? Let's begin the process of finding out.

Letting Go

Child asked Grandmother, 'What does it mean to reweave your life?' Grandmother answered, 'Unlearn your old harmful ways. Learn your new healing ways. Garden the stories you tell yourself.'

DR JAIYA JOHNS

The intention of Letting Go is to release the things that disempower you. Letting Go is about 'gardening' the beliefs or stories that we tell ourselves about the qualities of our true nature. The aspiration of this practice is to release ways of thinking that disempower us or weigh us down.

You may already have some sense for what these burdensome ways of thinking are, through the practices we have already covered. This practice brings more specific focus to current ways of thinking that make it hard to freely embody our best qualities.

Before you begin, select one of the qualities of your essential nature that you would like to feel a stronger connection with. It is advisable to start with a quality that does not feel completely out of your reach, but rather something you already feel you have some level of connection with.

In the practice below, I am using the quality of playfulness as an example. To practise, swap out the word 'playful' for the aspect of your essential nature you are focusing on. If focusing on your playfulness does not feel right for you, you might choose to focus instead on being compassionate, curious, confident, calm or creative.

LET'S PRACTISE

Begin by coming back to your senses. Focus your attention on one of your senses for three to five breaths.

What can you see, feel, taste, smell or hear?

As you begin to experience a sense of inner quieting, bring your attention to the quality you would like to embody more freely.

Next, complete the following sentence with the first thing that comes to mind:

'People who are playful are...'

If there is nothing critical about your response to the question, spend a few moments recalling a moment when you felt playful. How did it feel?

Take some deep breaths while imagining those feelings soaking into you, like cool rain soaking into dry, parched earth.

If you completed the sentence, 'People who are playful are...' in a critical way, spend a few moments reflecting on the following questions:

- What part of me believes this?
- What is this part of me afraid might happen if I were more playful?

- Where, when or how did this belief originate?
- When in the past have I enjoyed feeling naturally playful?
- What was that like for me?
- How might being more playful uplift me, those I work with and those I care about?
- What new possibilities might emerge from being more playful more often?

Finally, complete the sentence:

'If I had unshakable faith in my playful nature, I would...'

Don't forget to jot down anything you wish to remember and come back to.

Letting In

> *Renew thyself completely each day; do it*
> *again, and again, and forever again.*
> HENRY DAVID THOREAU

Our capacity to be the best we can be – to be courageous, creative, playful, calm and compassionate, is built on the foundation of our vitality. Our physical, mental and emotional wellbeing supports us to embody the qualities of our true nature.

The intention of this next aspect of the process, Letting In, is to fire up your life-force. This practice will increase your awareness of your core needs and help to clarify your non-negotiables – the things that you need to feel like yourself.

We have all heard the phrase 'running on empty', and we also know that we can't pour from an empty cup. But many people don't realise that we all have seven core needs[58] or seven 'cups' that need to be monitored and refilled to stay well. These cups may vary in size from person to person, but we all have the same set of seven.

These are your seven cups:

Connection
Your need for acceptance, belonging, affection, appreciation, love and community.

Physical wellbeing
Your need for nourishment, rest, sleep, safety, shelter and touch.

Honesty
Your need for authenticity, integrity and presence.

Play
Your need for joy, humour and light-heartedness.

Peace
Your need for harmony, ease, inspiration, order, equality and beauty.

Autonomy
Your need for freedom, choice, independence and spontaneity.

Meaning

Your need for contribution, growth, hope, learning, challenge, purpose and discovery.

Each cup represents a need that must be met for us to experience a sense of balance, fulfilment, happiness and health. When our cups are full, we have the strength, motivation and energy we need to embody the most vibrant expression of all we are. And when our seven core needs are not met, we can find ourselves in survival mode with our best qualities way out of our reach.

For example, one of my biggest needs is for physical wellbeing. When I don't feel physically fit and strong, I don't like myself. So, I have learned over the years that I really need to prioritise exercise. My early morning HIIT sessions and my weekend yoga class are non-negotiables for me. If I'm unable to exercise for a few days, I just don't feel like myself.

One of the biggest challenges I see with many corporate wellbeing programs is that they make big assumptions about what people most need to thrive. Only you can determine the best way to fill each of your seven cups.

Here are a few examples of non-negotiables my coaching clients have identified – these are the things they need in their lives to feel like themselves:

- Playing tennis with my mates on Thursday nights

- Taking my son to his swimming lesson
- Walking my dog on the beach in the morning
- Playing my guitar
- Date nights with my wife (without the kids!)
- Spending time in nature
- Fishing on the lake on weekends
- Volunteering at a local charity that is close to my heart

LET'S PRACTISE

Begin by coming back to your senses. Focus your attention on one of your senses for three to five breaths.

What can you see, feel, taste, smell or hear?

As you begin to experience a sense of inner quieting, I invite you to read back through the above list of core needs and reflect on the following questions:

- What is the relative size of each of my cups? (You might like to draw them.)
- How full (or empty) is each of my cups right now?
- What fills each of my cups?
- What drains each of my cups?
- What is getting in the way of me taking better care of myself?
- Considering all of this, what are the things I need in my life (or out of my life) to feel more like myself?

- What are my non-negotiables?
- How might honouring my non-negotiables uplift me, those I work with and those I care about?
- What is my next best step?

Finally, don't forget to jot down anything you wish to remember and come back to.

Letting Be

The intention of Letting Be is to freely allow the expression of your essential nature.

Letting Be is not about assertion; it's about allowance. It's about no longer trying to suppress the qualities of your true nature, but, rather, learning how to trust in their ability to lift you. Letting Be allows the qualities of your true nature to just *be there*, unimpeded and unrestrained.

This practice works well in moments when you feel stuck or unsure about the best path forwards.

LET'S PRACTISE

Begin by coming back to your senses. Focus your attention on one of your senses for three to five breaths.

What can you see, feel, taste, smell or hear?

As you begin to experience a sense of inner quieting, bring your attention to the area in your life where you currently feel a little stuck.

Next, reflect on the following questions:

- In this moment, how might I extend my care towards the parts of myself that feel somehow unsure, vulnerable, exposed or afraid?
- In the context of this challenge, what would it mean to be my true self?
- What is my next best step?
- As I move forward, how might I continue to take good care of the parts of myself that feel unsure, vulnerable, exposed or afraid?

Finally, don't forget to jot down anything you wish to remember and come back to.

PRACTICE 5:

Harnessing your essence

There is a vitality, a life-force, an energy, a quickening that is translated through you into action, and because there is only one of you in all of time, this expression is unique. And if you block it, it will never exist through any other medium and it will be lost. The world will not have it. It is not your business to determine how good it is nor how valuable nor how it compares with other expressions. It is your business to keep it yours, clearly and directly, to keep the channel open.

MARTHA GRAHAM

The fifth and final practice we're going to play with is the practice of connecting to your essence. The intention of this practice is to tap into a powerful, inner, sustainable source of energy and vitality that has the potential to uplift you, those you lead and those you love.

WHY PRACTISE?

A client who works in HR recently shared the following insight in one of my group coaching sessions: 'When I am being myself, I have enough energy to do anything, but when I am not being myself, everything feels hard.'

Many of us fuel our working lives through energy sources that come from outside us. These energy sources include trying to prove something to someone (or everyone), trying to win against someone (or everyone), or trying to appease, please, be liked or be perfect by comparing ourselves to some ever-elusive external standard of worthiness. When we find ourselves running on the fumes, we may turn to harsh self-criticism or to caffeine, sugar and other stimulants to 'soldier on'.

Sure, we experience an energy surge when we are being propelled by a part's desire to prove themself, to compete or to achieve their way to worthiness. These energy surges can certainly be powerful, but they are not sustainable. They take a heavy toll on our wellbeing and our relationships; they impede our long-term performance and are likely to create collateral damage.

I know these 'dirty' energy sources all too well. For too many years of my corporate career I was fuelled by unhealthy striving and proving. I have been sucked into a narrow definition of success in the past that did not work for me or for my family – an exhausting ladder-climbing-at-any-cost mindset. I was propelled by a dangerous belief that if I could achieve enough and do enough, I would finally feel like I was enough. This fuel source was also powerful, but in no way sustainable. Looking back, I can see that this way of being was heavily polluting for my body, my mind, my relationships – and (ironically) my leadership. Today, I am powered by a sustainable energy source. I know how to amplify and harness my **essence** as a playful, passionate change activator.

When we are aligned with our essential nature, we feel uplifted and alive. We experience authentic empowerment. It becomes possible not only to love what we do, but also to love *(or at least like)* who we're being while we do it.

Recently, my good friend and former coaching client Jasmine shared a heart-warming post on LinkedIn. I was so thrilled to read Jasmine's post that I cried happy tears and called her immediately. Jasmine has kindly given me permission to share her post here:

> *Traditionally (and generationally), many of us have performed and motivated ourselves through fear, shame, scarcity.*
>
> *This has cost us dearly – illness (physical and mental), burn-out, poor relationships, addictions, unethical behaviour, the list goes on.*
>
> *But there is an opportunity to change energy sources and choose love, trust, faith, hope, purpose, meaning – clean and renewable energy sources to fuel our performance.*
>
> *Many of us fear that the moment we switch energy sources, we'll stop performing because that's what we've always known and done. But is that true?*

I have experimented with this in my running. I used to taunt, criticise, belittle and judge myself as I was running. Sure, it got me running a little faster, but it never felt good, and I wasn't enjoying the journey.

When Cassandra Goodman, as my coach, challenged my inner game and invited me to consider an alternative energy source – a kind, encouraging, loving and curious inner energy source, I was sceptical.

But I agreed to try it – just once!

I would be kind to myself during my next run.

Well, that is when I soared.

I did a Personal Best that same weekend. I kept getting PBs.

I then ran a half marathon.

And most importantly, now I LOVE running and I miss it when I am unable to do it.

Jasmine could never have predicted where changing the way she spoke to herself would take her. She recently completed a full marathon. Small, gentle changes in the way you relate to yourself and to your parts can have a profound ripple effect. By tapping into your essence, you access a pure, powerful, renewable energy source.

HOW TO PRACTISE

There are three parts to the practice of reconnecting to your essence as a source of uplifting energy. The intention of these practices is to allow the qualities of your essential nature to energise you and uplift your performance, just like they did for Jasmine.

Part 1: Understanding your current energy sources

In the first part, I will guide you to increase your awareness of your current sources of energy – along with their impact and sustainability.

LET'S PRACTISE

Begin by coming back to your senses. Focus your attention on one of your senses for three to five breaths.

What can you see, feel, taste, smell or hear?

As you begin to experience a sense of inner quieting, reflect on the following questions:

- What currently drives me at work?
- What are the benefits of how I've been working?
- What might be the unintended consequences of how I've been working?
- What's the true cost of how I've been working?
- If I were to continue to work in the same way for the next year, what might be the likely outcomes for me, my colleagues and those I care most about?

Finally, don't forget to jot down anything you wish to remember and come back to.

Part 2: Discovering your essence

The intention of the second part of the practice is to improve your awareness of your essence. It can be tricky to get a sense for our true essence. I often find that people can beautifully describe the unique energy of a colleague or friend, but their own essence is invisible to them.

To help, I am going to invite you to work through a range of prompts and questions. Focus on the questions and prompts that work for you and leave the rest. Capture your answers without over-thinking it. When you have finished, read back through all your answers to identify emerging themes – and you'll be well on your way to really understanding your unique essence.

LET'S PRACTISE

Begin by coming back to your senses. Focus your attention on one of your senses for three to five breaths.

What can you see, feel, taste, smell or hear?

As you begin to experience a sense of inner quieting, reflect on some (or all) of the following questions:

- What makes my heart sing?
- What makes me feel fully alive and activated?
- What sparks joy for me?
- How would my closest friends describe me?
- What have past colleagues written on farewell cards?
- What does my pet see in me?
- Who is the 'me' that emerges in moments of loving presence?
- How am I being when I'm being most myself?

Next, complete some (or all) of the following prompts:

- I feel most myself when...
- What I know to be true about myself is...
- If you really knew me, you would know that...
- I am unique because of the way I...
- People sometimes tell me that they love my...
- People sometimes tell me that they really appreciate my...
- It would feel so good to be able to show the world more of my...

Finally, don't forget to jot down anything you wish to remember and come back to.

Part 3: Reclaiming your truth

The third part of this final practice is to use the themes that have emerged to create some powerful 'I am' statements. The purpose of these statements is to anchor you back to your most positive and powerful ways of being as a TRUE leader. The idea is to have a simple way to remind yourself of the person you choose to be. You can do this by silently repeating to yourself three to five 'I am' statements in moments that matter.

I have a beautiful friend called Kate. The essence of Kate is a blend of calm, caring and grace. Kate is also someone who is very brave. And so, Kate's practice of connecting to her essence might involve quieting her mind and dropping into her body in a way that feels right for her and silently reminding herself: *I am calm. I am caring. I am graceful. I am brave.*

To ease into the practice, you might find it helpful to look at a photo of yourself when you were little – perhaps between the ages of three and five years old. In the practice guidance below, I have included statements you can try on for size. It is important that, over time, you create your own statements that reflect the qualities of your true essence.

LET'S PRACTISE

Begin by coming back to your senses. Focus your attention on one of your senses for three to five breaths.

What can you see, feel, taste, smell or hear?

As you begin to experience a sense of inner quieting, try reading out the below statements, noticing how it feels:

- I am caring
- I am creative
- I am playful
- I am confident
- I am curious
- I am wise
- I am capable
- I am powerful
- I am worthy
- I am brave
- I am not alone
- I am safe
- I am supported
- I am protected
- I am seen
- I am free
- I am loved
- I belong

Now, create some 'I am' statements of your own.

CONCLUSION

When I'm being true to my deepest self,
it doesn't really cause harm to anybody.
It actually serves the greatest good.

TARA BRACH

The day I deeply committed to being true to myself started off like any other day. It was a warm Saturday morning. The smell of jasmine was in the air and I was in my standard weekend active wear. It had been a particularly challenging week at work. The corporate environment I was working in at the time was heavy with fear and greed-fuelled politics, and I could feel myself being pulled way, way out of alignment with my true nature.

I was walking to my car from the supermarket, arms laden with groceries, when I saw it – a small ornate sign on the footpath that said in curly red letters, 'Tattoo Parlour, Walk-Ins Welcome'.

Suddenly, something crystallised inside me.

Within seconds I was standing inside a portal to another world. A humming, buzzing world filled with dark, beautiful things. A world inhabited by people who make big, lasting commitments. People who boldly embody the message: This is who I am.

'Um, hello … How much does a tattoo cost? And how long does it take?'

The rapid-fire answer was, '$120. We'll have you out of here in forty minutes.'

Clearly, I was not the first slightly desperate-looking middle-aged mum to be pulled through their doors like a moth to a flame.

'Okay! Just give me a minute.'

I stepped back outside into the bright sunlight and dug up my phone from the bottom of my bag. The telephone conversation with my husband went something like this:

Me: Hi, I'm going to be a bit late getting home with the groceries.

Him: Okay, everything all right?

Me: Yeah, um … I'm just going to get a tattoo.

Silence.

Him: What?

Me: Don't worry, it's just a small one, a little star on my wrist.

Him: Ah, okay.

Me: I just need a reminder, something visible. I really think it will help.

Him: Okay then – if you're really sure … But you are going to have to deal with the kids when they tell us that they want a tattoo.

Honestly, I was not sure if I was doing the right thing, even though I would never have admitted that to my husband at the time. Despite the voices of doubt, I decided to have faith in my own knowing that getting a small star permanently etched into my left wrist was somehow my next best step.

And I am so glad I did.

I love my little North Star tattoo and the commitment, non-conformity and spontaneous activism it symbolises. I have since learned that the Latin root of the word desire is *desidere*, meaning 'of the stars'. My tattoo is a permanent reminder of my highest desires: to figure out how to live a life that's true to myself even when it's hard, and to generously share what I learn with others.

My kids are still young enough to think that my tattoo is cool and, so far, they have not asked when they can get one. My hope is that they will never need one. My hope is that they grow up with an unbroken line of sight to their uniqueness. And that they have a strong awareness of who they are at their core, and lasting relationships with the parts of themselves they need to take care of. That they stay brave enough to stand out rather than fit in and let their true colours shine.

Now, that would be *really* cool.

By remembering and reconnecting to our deepest, truest selves, we liberate our highest potential and serve the greatest good. We open ourselves to new possibilities in our professional and personal lives.

The more you put the concepts you have learned in this book into practice, the more you'll uplift your performance, and feel more fulfilment, happiness and vitality. You'll give inner and outer peace a chance.

The practices you have learned will support you to rekindle, celebrate and honour your most important and enduring relationship – the relationship you have with yourself. By changing the relationship you have with yourself, you'll change the relationships you have with all others.

Many of the leaders I work with recoil at the idea of loving themselves. They feel it is clichéd, self-indulgent and unrealistic. Not everyone feels safe enough to fall in love with anyone, let alone themselves. Some people need to step into love. I hope that *Being True* has seeded the possibility of cultivating love towards yourself, step by tender step.

I encourage you to continue to play, to adjust and to adapt the practices you have learned. Please make them your own. I hope that you find yourself continuing to come back to them for many years to come.

I define self-fidelity as the practice of being true to our essential nature. If there were a vow of self-fidelity, it might go something like this:

> *I promise to care for and honour all parts of myself in good times and in bad, in sickness and in health, for better and for worse.*

I promise to trust in the truth of my worthiness, the importance of my uniqueness and the vastness of my potential.

But above all else, I promise to practise remembering who I truly am, undeterred by my perpetual forgetfulness.

The more I work with brave, big-hearted leaders who are pioneering the practices of *Being True* in their workplaces and homes, the more I get a clear sense for how they can powerfully guide us to be good leaders and good humans. And the more I understand their potential to uplift our working lives.

No matter how far you have drifted away from your core, it's never too late to remember and honour the truth of who you are.

I sincerely hope that you enjoy your onward journey inwards and upwards. I would love to stay in touch.

Support

Put down the weight of your aloneness,
and ease into the conversation.
DAVID WHYTE

I believe that now more than ever, we must reconnect to the truth of who we are as a catalyst for the co-creation of workplaces where people can thrive, perform and belong.

While the pilgrimage of figuring out how to honour the truest expression of who we are is deeply personal in nature, there can be so many benefits to travelling in the company of others. I established The Centre for Self-Fidelity to connect, support and inspire a growing global community of self-fidelity pioneers.

It is my hope that, over time, the practice of self-fidelity becomes as well respected as the practice of self-compassion. My dream is to see the word self-fidelity added to the dictionary in my lifetime.

As we restore faith in ourselves, we restore faith in each other.

Ease Into The Conversation

One of my greatest joys is facilitating honest conversations with like-minded, big-hearted leaders united in their desire to be true to themselves, and give others permission to do the same so that workplaces become safer spaces for everyone.

One-on-one coaching is something I also offer and love to do.

If you would like to learn more about my individual and group coaching programs, visit **self-fidelity.com.**

Discover Additional Resources

Visit **self-fidelity.com** to discover a range of valuable additional resources, including a free printable *Being True Playbook* and a free *Overwhelm Survival Guide.*

You can also subscribe to my blog (**self-fidelity.com/blog**), where I regularly share new ideas on the small, practical steps you can take to be more yourself at work.

The IFS Institute (**ifs-institute.com**) also offers a wide range of articles and other valuable resources. If you're curious to learn more about Internal Family Systems, Dr Richard Schwartz's wonderful book *No Bad Parts* is a great place to start.

Spread The Word

If you enjoyed my book and would like to help others discover the simple principles and practices that support us to be true to ourselves, use **#beingtrue** to spread the word.

Client Feedback

'Cassie delivered a workshop to 450 of our employees. I was totally mesmerised by Cassie's engagement style and content. Her story telling skills are exemplary.'

ANNA ANDREONI, SENIOR LEARNING & DEVELOPMENT ADVISOR, ORIGIN ENERGY

'The work of tending to my mental health can feel quite lonely. Your group coaching program has helped me to realise that I am not alone. As a result, I am far more motivated to keep going with putting small changes into practice.'

KATE JARVIS, CLIMATE FINANCE SPECIALIST, ASIAN DEVELOPMENT BANK

'I loved reading your books but participating in your program has taken my understanding of what it really means to be true to myself to a whole new level.'

MELISSA BUCKINGHAM, PEOPLE EXPERIENCE DESIGNER, LEAPGEN

'I completed Cassie's Leadership Development Program over a year ago and it has had such a lasting impact on me. An even more powerful catalyst was the small, simple changes I made. I now refer to these as an effortless snowball of transformative practices connecting me with my true self.'

SALLY PEDLOW, HEAD OF PEOPLE (PHARMACY & COMPOUNDING), ICON GROUP

'*Your program provides a great framework that helps us to be true to ourselves. I discovered that even if we work in high pressure environments, we can still be playful and bring joy! Thank you! I would highly recommend your program to other leaders.*'

DR NADIA CHAVES, INFECTIOUS DISEASES
AND INTERNAL MEDICINE SPECIALIST

'*Cassie is an authentic and intuitive coach. Above all, Cassie cares deeply for those she serves, without reservation or judgement.*'

WILLIAM SHEFFIELD, CHIEF PEOPLE OFFICER,
WESTFUND HEALTH INSURANCE

'*Receiving coaching from Cassie has been a game-changer for me. Her knowledge and experience combined with her genuine ability to connect with people makes her an ideal coach. It is an absolutely privilege to be coached by her.*'

JESSIE WADDELL, ORGANISATIONAL DEVELOPMENT AND
COMMUNICATIONS PROFESSIONAL

Acknowledgements

Books are funny things to create. They start off as one thing, but as you get going, they turn out to be something else entirely. It's kind of like giving birth. Except you don't know whether you're bringing a boy, a girl or a unicorn into the world.

One thing is for sure – it takes a team to create a good book, and so I have so many people I would like to acknowledge and thank.

Firstly, I would like to thank Dr Richard Schwartz for bringing IFS to the world. It has changed my life and the lives of so many.

I would like to extend my heart-felt thanks to all the wonderful clients who have trusted me to guide them on their experiences of inner exploration. The profound nature of your discoveries and the tremendous privilege of bearing witness to your self-healing have been truly extraordinary. Your courage is what inspires me to keep writing and sharing, even when part of me feels unsure, inadequate and overwhelmed.

Thank you to my husband, Andrew, and my two sons, Elliot and Zach, for encouraging me and for being understanding when I needed quiet writing time. Special thanks to Elliot for helping with the first edit of my manuscript and for sharing his special gift of finding exactly the right words. Special thanks to Zach for being such a wonderful coach, and for encouraging me to believe in myself and to care less about what other people think.

Thanks to my mum and dad for your continuous and loving support.

To my wonderful friends Carolyn Howard, Jasmine Malki, Kate Jarvis, Elise Morris, Kellee Lewis, Ingrid Just, Andy Pert, Ainsley Jeffery, Fi Mims, Mei Ouw, Johanna Nelson, Lizzie Townsend, Hayley Dragun, Marlene Harris, Ming Chan, Melissa Buckingham and Renata Bernarde – thank you for your patient and kind encouragement.

Scott MacMillan, Olivia Joerges, Carolyn Jackson, Julia Kuris and the talented team at Grammar Factory Publishing, thank you for your exceptional support.

Thanks also to Sandy Grant, Courtney Nicholls, at the wonderful team at Hardie Grant for believing in me and in *Being True*.

Kelly Irving and the fabulous Expert Author Academy community, thank you for many years of support, and camaraderie.

Richard Brisebois, thank you for believing in my vision for The Centre for Self-Fidelity and for sharing your wisdom and expertise with me so generously.

Mia Bowyer, thank you for enabling me to aim higher with my mission.

Thank you to the early manuscript reviewers for your honest feedback – Kate Jarvis, Mark Evarts, Ingrid Just, Kellee Lewis, Kellie King, Allie Mackay, Melissa Buckingham, Georgie Cooke, Bron Reed, Mohini Sashindranath, Carly Moulang, Karen Stein and Briar Harte.

Jasmine Malki, thank you for giving me permission to share your inspiring story.

Arianna Huffington, Agapi Stassinopoulos, Alex Christou, Carly Moulang and the whole team at Thrive Global, thank you for your inspiration and support.

Ellen Airey, thank you for introducing me to IFS. Our conversation all those years ago was the spark that started this book.

Thanks to Selma, Rhea, Mick, Marsha and the fabulous crew at CoWork Me St Kilda for all you do to support me and The Centre for Self-Fidelity.

Thanks Fi Mims for helping me to shine through authentic and consistent personal branding.

Thank you Julie Griffiths and the team at Tighten Up St Kilda for supporting me to build the strength and stamina I needed to get this book over the line.

Dr Rick Hanson, thank you for your support, encouragement and wise teachings.

Dr Stuart Brown, thank you for teaching me about my innate, playful nature and for your inspiration and encouragement.

Tony and Donna, thank you for opening your home to me when I needed space to bunker down and write without distraction.

Thank you to the many wonderful members of the IFS community who have supported me – especially Georgie Cooke, Allie Mackay and Simon d'Orsogna.

About the Author

Cassandra Goodman is the founder and director of The Centre for Self-Fidelity.

Cassandra's career has moved further and further up the supply chain from customer experience transformation to employee experience transformation to transforming the inner experiences of leaders.

Through her coaching, training, speaking, consulting and writing, Cassandra supports busy, big-hearted leaders to be true to themselves as a catalyst for the co-creation of workplaces where people can thrive, perform and belong.

Cassandra brings over three decades of business experience to her work and has held a range of senior leadership roles, including Global Director of Employee Experience at a healthcare company where she helped to activate the organisation's purpose, 'Longer, Healthier, Happier Lives,' for their 86,000 employees around the world.

Cassandra is an IFS-informed coach. She has a master coaching certification and is an accredited Thrive Global Executive Coach. She is also an accredited Lean Six Sigma Master Black Belt (and no, she can't catch flies with chopsticks).

Cassandra was born in Sydney, Australia and currently lives in Melbourne.

This is her second book.

Learn more at **self-fidelity.com**

Connect with Cassandra on:

in linkedin.com/in/cassandra-goodman

self.fidelity.cassandragoodman

Endnotes

1 Took-pa Turner. (2017). Belonging: Remembering ourselves home. Her OwnRoomPress;

2 Evan W. Carr, Andrew Reece, Gabriella Rosen Kellerman, and Alexi Robichaux. (2019, December 16). The value of belonging at work. Harvard Business Review. Retrieved October 16, 2022, from https://hbr.org/2019/12/the-value-of-belonging-at-work

3 Cecelia Herbert. (2021, December 9). Workplace belonging: How to increase employee engagement in 2022. Qualtrics. Retrieved October 16, 2022, from https://www.qualtrics.com/blog/belonging-at-work/

4 Dina Pozzo, Courage in the lucky country – A perspective on Australian organisations. Leading with courage. (2021, March 3). Retrieved October 16, 2022, from https://leadingwithcourage.com.au/210223-dare-to-discover/

5 Evan W. Carr, Andrew Reece, Gabriella Rosen Kellerman, and Alexi Robichaux. (2019, December 16). The value of belonging at work. Harvard Business Review. Retrieved October 16, 2022, from https://hbr.org/2019/12/the-value-of-belonging-at-work

6 Kathryn Jacob, Sue Unerman, Mark Edwards (2022). Belonging: The key to transforming and maintaining diversity, inclusion and equality at work. Bloomsbury Business.

7 Francesca Gino, Ovul Sezer, Laura Huang. (2020, June 12). To be or not to be your authentic self? Organizational Behavior and Human Decision Processes. Retrieved October 16, 2022, from https://www.sciencedirect.com/science/article/abs/pii/S0749597817308865

8 Richard C. Schwartz, Ph.D et al www.ifs-institute.com

9 The C-suite's role in well-being. (2022, August 3). Deloitte United States. Retrieved October 16, 2022, from https://www2.deloitte.com/us/en/pages/about-deloitte/articles/the-c-suite-role-in-well-being.html

10 Jay Bevington, Shagun Ahuja, Hiba Hage Obeid, Karim Mokdad. Well-being at the heart of the employee experience for the Social Enterprise. (2021, March 23). Deloitte. Retrieved October 16, 2022, from https://www2.deloitte.com/xe/en/pages/human-capital/articles/well-being-heart-employee-experience-social-enterprise.html

11 The C-suite's role in well-being. (2022, August 3). Deloitte United States. Retrieved October 16, 2022, from https://www2.deloitte.com/us/en/pages/about-deloitte/articles/the-c-suite-role-in-well-being.html

12 The Wellbeing Lab Workplace Report. Australian HR Institute & The Wellbeing Lab. (2022, April 6). Retrieved October 16, 2022, from https://www.ahri.com.au/resources/hr-research/the-wellbeing-lab-workplace-report

13 Sutton, A. (2020). Living the good life: A meta-analysis of authenticity, well-being and engagement. Personality and Individual Differences. 153, 109645. https://doi.org/10.1016/j.paid.2019.109645

14 Francesca Gino, Maryam Kouchaki, Adam D. Galinsky (2019, May 10). Fake it until you make it? not so fast. Kellogg Insight. Retrieved October 16, 2022, from https://insight.kellogg.northwestern.edu/article/the-problem-with-faking-it

15 Smet, A. D., Dowling, B., Mugayar-Baldocchi, M., Schaninger, B. (2022, March 28). 'Great attrition' or 'great attraction'? the choice is yours. McKinsey & Company. Retrieved October 16, 2022, from https://www.mckinsey.com/capabilities/people-and-organizational-performance/our-insights/great-attrition-or-great-attraction-the-choice-is-yours

16 Adam Grant "Granted" newsletter, August 2022

17 Smet, A. D., Dowling, B., Mugayar-Baldocchi, M., Schaninger, B. (2022, March 28). 'Great attrition' or 'great attraction'? the choice is yours. McKinsey & Company; Company. Retrieved October 16, 2022, from https://www.mckinsey.com/capabilities/people-and-organizational-performance/our-insights/great-attrition-or-great-attraction-the-choice-is-yours

18 Brown, B. (2017, September 11). Finding our way to true belonging. ideas.ted.com. Retrieved October 16, 2022, from https://ideas.ted.com/finding-our-way-to-true-belonging/

19 Kathryn Jacob, Sue Unerman, Mark Edwards (2022). Belonging: The key to transforming and maintaining diversity, inclusion and equality at work. Bloomsbury Business.

20 Licata, M. (2020). A healing space: Befriending ourselves in Difficult Times. Sounds True.

21 Arruda, W. (2017, December 12). What employees really think about their bosses. Forbes. Retrieved October 16, 2022, from https://www.forbes.com/sites/williamarruda/2017/12/12/what-employees-really-think-about-their-boss/

22 Schwartz, R. (2021). No bad parts: Healing trauma and restoring wholeness with the internal family systems model. Sounds True, Incorporated.

23 Schwartz, R. (n.d.). The Internal Family Systems Model Outline. IFS Institute. Retrieved October 16, 2022, from https://ifs-institute.com/resources/articles/internal-family-systems-model-outline

24 S Tsabary, (Dr), Oprah's SuperSoul Conversations Podcast, 'Dr. Shefali Tsabary: The awakened life', 2019.

25 What self-awareness really is (and how to cultivate it). Harvard Business Review. (2018, January 4). Retrieved October 16, 2022, from https://hbr.org/2018/01/what-self-awareness-really-is-and-how-to-cultivate-it

26　5 REASONS You Feel Lost In Life & How To Find Yourself. Brené Brown & Lewis Howes, 26 Jul 2021, YouTube https://www.youtube.com/watch?v=vCpYHYmHHvY

27　5 REASONS You Feel Lost In Life & How To Find Yourself. Brené Brown & Lewis Howes, 26 Jul 2021, YouTube https://www.youtube.com/watch?v=vCpYHYmHHvY

28　H D Thoreau, Walden: Or, life in the woods, New York, United States: Dover Publications Inc., 1995.

29　Wikimedia Foundation. (2020, March 16). Dunning-kruger effect. Wikipedia. Retrieved October 16, 2022, from https://en.wikipedia.org/wiki/Dunning-Kruger_effect

30　Eurich, T. (2018). Insight: The surprising truth about how others see us, how we see ourselves, and why the answers matter more than we think. Currency.

31　Morgan, J. (2021, August 21). Internal versus external self-awareness. Medium. Retrieved October 16, 2022, from https://jacobm.medium.com/internal-versus-external-self-awareness-c17cc68fc94e

32　Discovering your authentic leadership. Harvard Business Review. (2007, February). Retrieved October 16, 2022, from https://hbr.org/2007/02/discovering-your-authentic-leadership

33　Tasha Eurich. What self-awareness really is (and how to cultivate it). Harvard Business Review. (2018, January 4). Retrieved October 16, 2022, from https://hbr.org/2018/01/what-self-awareness-really-is-and-how-to-cultivate-it

34　Silvia, P. J., O'Brien, M. E. (2004). Self-awareness and constructive functioning: Revisiting "The human dilemma." Journal of Social and Clinical Psychology, 23(4), 475–489. https://doi.org/10.1521/jscp.23.4.475.40307

35　Luthans, F., Peterson, S. J. (2003). 360-degree feedback with systematic coaching: Empirical analysis suggests a winning combination. Human Resource Management, 42(3), 243–256. https://doi.org/10.1002/hrm.10083

36 A Better Return on Self-Awareness. (2013, August). A better return on self-awareness. Korn Ferry. Retrieved October 16, 2022, from https://www.kornferry.com/institute/647-a-better-return-on-self-awareness

37 Tasha Eurich. What self-awareness really is (and how to cultivate it). Harvard Business Review. (2018, January 4). Retrieved October 16, 2022, from https://hbr.org/2018/01/what-self-awareness-really-is-and-how-to-cultivate-it

38 Schwartz, R. (2021). No bad parts: Healing trauma and restoring wholeness with the internal family systems model. Sounds True, Incorporated.

39 Team, G. T. E. (2018, December 2). Internal Family Systems (IFS). Internal Family Systems Therapy. Retrieved October 16, 2022, from https://www.goodtherapy.org/learn-about-therapy/types/internal-family-systems-therapy

40 Schwartz, R., Sweezy, M. (2020). Internal Family Systems therapy. Guilford Press.

41 Schwartz, R. (2021). No bad parts: Healing trauma and restoring wholeness with the internal family systems model. Sounds True, Incorporated.

42 Essence discovery. Carol Sanford. (n.d.). Retrieved October 16, 2022, from https://carolsanford.com/essence-discovery/

43 Dissociative identity disorder: What is it, symptoms & treatment. Cleveland Clinic. (n.d.). Retrieved October 16, 2022, from https://my.clevelandclinic.org/health/diseases/9792-dissociative-identity-disorder-multiple-personality-disorder

44 Schwartz, R. (n.d.). The Internal Family Systems Model Outline. IFS Institute. Retrieved October 16, 2022, from https://ifs-institute.

com/resources/articles/internal-family-systems-model-outline

45 Took-pa Turner. (2017). Belonging: Remembering ourselves home. Her Own Room Press;

46 Dr Gabor Maté. The Wisdom Of Trauma -. (2022, August 19). Retrieved October 16, 2022, from https://thewisdomoftrauma.com/resources/

47 Schwartz, R. C., & Sweezy, M. (2020). Internal Family Systems therapy. Guilford Press.

48 Schwartz, R. (n.d.). The Internal Family Systems Model Outline. IFS Institute. Retrieved October 16, 2022, from https://ifs-institute.com/resources/articles/internal-family-systems-model-outline

49 Licata, M. (2020). A healing space: Befriending ourselves in Difficult Times. Sounds True.

50 B Sutton-Smith, Psychology Today, 'What's the opposite of play?', April 05, 2016, www.psychologytoday.com/au/blog/conceptual-revolution/201604/what-s-the-opposite-play

51 S Brown, (Dr), Play: How it shapes the brain, opens the imagination and invigorates the soul, New York: United States: Penguin Putnam Inc, 2010.

52 Wheatley, Margaret. J. (2017). Who do we choose to be?: Facing reality, claiming leadership, Restoring Sanity. Berrett-Koehler Publishers, Inc.

53 Riemersma, J. (2020). Altogether you: Experiencing personal and spiritual transformation with Internal Family Systems therapy. Pivotal Press.

54 Schwartz, R. (2021). No bad parts: Healing trauma and restoring wholeness with the internal family systems model. Sounds True, Incorporated.

55 IFS Institute – IFS Online Circle –with Richard Schwartz, Pamela Krause and Toni Herbine-Blank. https://ifs-institute.com/trainings

56 Schwartz, R. C., & Sweezy, M. (2020). Internal Family Systems therapy. Guilford Press.

57 Hanson, R., & Hanson, F. (2020). Resilient: How to grow an unshakable core of calm, strength, and happiness. Harmony Books.

58 Needs inventory. Center for Nonviolent Communication. (n.d.). Retrieved October 16, 2022, from https://www.cnvc.org/training/resource/needs-inventory